PAINTING
Luscious
FRUIT

Elizabeth Hayes, CDA

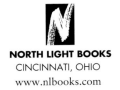

NORTH LIGHT BOOKS
CINCINNATI, OHIO
www.nlbooks.com

About the Author

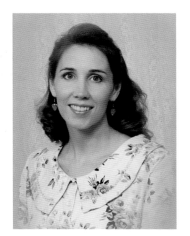

Elizabeth Hayes grew up in an artistic environment. Her grandmother taught her how to crochet, do needlepoint and play the piano. Her mother was a professional singer, her father did some painting and her older brother sculpted. Elizabeth credits her mother with introducing her to decorative art. "I'd always considered myself an artistic and creative person and had taken art classes in college, but it wasn't until my mother and I attended a seminar at Cedar Crest [Kansas] that I knew where my artistic abilities would take me."

Elizabeth is a successful travel teacher and author of four previous decorative art books. She is a Certified Decorative Artist (CDA) with the Society of Decorative Painters. Elizabeth describes herself as a person with an insatiable passion for painting. "I believe this is a God-given talent and my desire to create something beautiful can only come from Him."

In addition to painting, Elizabeth enjoys gardening, playing the piano and anything science fiction.

Elizabeth, her husband, Don, and their three children, Brittney, Justin and Brooke, live in Pittsburgh, Pennsylvania. Write to Elizabeth at 428 Cadberry Court, Pittsburgh, Pennsylvania 15241, or E-mail her at Ehdesigns@aol.com. Visit her Web site at www.elizabethhayes.com.

Other fine North Light Books are available from your local bookstore, art supply store or direct from the publisher.

04 03 02 01 00   5 4 3 2 1

Library of Congress Cataloging-in-Publication Data

Hayes, Elizabeth
    Painting luscious fruit / Elizabeth Hayes.
        p.   cm.
    Includes index.
    ISBN 1-58180-078-9 (pbk. : alk. paper)—ISBN 1-58180-083-5 (pob : alk. paper)
    1. Fruit in art. 2. Painting--Technique. I. Title.
ND1400 . H39 2000
751.45'434--dc21   00-022016

Editor: Jennifer Long
Production Coordinator: Emily Gross
Designer: Mary Barnes Clark and Wendy Dunning
Production Artist: Jennifer Dailey
Step-by-step photography: Christine Polomsky
Finished project photography: Al Parrish

Dedication

This book would not be possible were it not for my learning experiences from teaching. I have learned more from critiquing my students' paintings than I ever thought possible. So, to all the students who have put their faith in me as a teacher, thank you for making me stretch beyond my current skills.

To my family—thank you for understanding that I like to paint much more than I like to cook.

To my Monday morning painting buddy, Patti—thanks for always being there and for making Mondays so much fun.

Acknowledgments

Many thanks to Winsor & Newton and Delta for supplying the paints used in this book.

Thank you to Gretchen Cagle, PCM Studios, Carolyn's Folk Art Studio, The Pesky Bear, Cooper's Works, Wayne's WoodenWare and Barb Watson for graciously supplying the surfaces on which I painted.

Thank you to Kathy Kipp, Jenny Long and Christine Polomsky from North Light Books for having faith in me and making this a very rewarding experience.

Thank you to Robert Daley who always has such an interesting way of critiquing my work and for making me think that I actually have some talent.

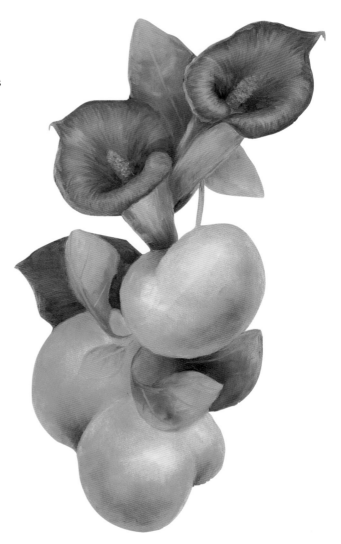

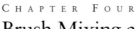
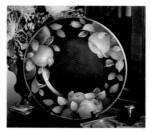
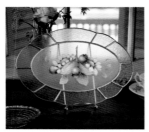
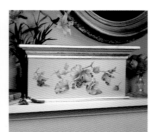
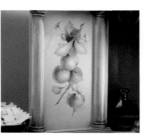
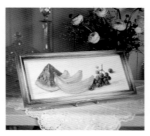
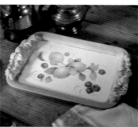
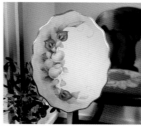
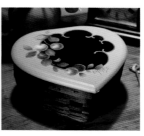
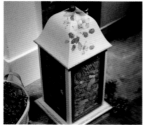
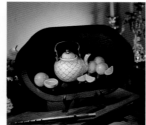
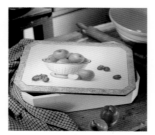
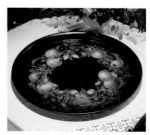

PROJECT 1
Blueberries and Daisies...26

PROJECT 2
Plums and Blossoms...36

PROJECT 3
Watermelon, Bananas and Grapes...44

PROJECT 4
Cherries...54

PROJECT 5
Apples All Around...60

PROJECT 6
Grapes and Poppies...68

PROJECT 7
Lemons and Strawberries...76

PROJECT 8
Peaches and Calla Lilies...84

PROJECT 9
Raspberries and Dogwoods...92

PROJECT 10
Orange Tea...100

PROJECT 11
Apples in a Colander...110

PROJECT 12
Fruit Wreath...118

I actually started my painting career working in acrylics, but when I took my first oil class I was instantly converted. I prefer oils to acrylics for several reasons:

❧ First, I love the open time that you have with oils. I love to have time to blend and work from one area to another without the fear of the paint drying too fast.

❧ I love to play around on my palette, creating subtle changes in value and temperature with my mixes. I can't do this with acrylics because they dry too fast and they don't react the same way as oils when mixing.

❧ I love the richness that comes from oils that you can't quite get with acrylics.

❧ Finally, I only need a basic palette of ten to twelve colors to create any color under the rainbow. (I can work with fewer colors, but I find that my twelve basic colors help me mix a wide range of colors and values.)

With acrylics I need to buy new bottles of paint with every project. I literally have buckets filled with acrylic paint. This creates a storage problem, on top of the enormous cost involved with buying new paint every time you sit down to paint a new project.

With oils, I simply lay out my same ten to twelve colors and begin painting. I never have to wonder if I have the correct color on hand because I know I can mix it.

A Note on the Format of This Book

As you progress through the projects in this book, you will learn new techniques and build your skills.

Project one deals with the basic elements of painting. Each project in succession touches on a new technique that will help you in your development as an artist.

If you want to just paint one or two projects from this book, that is fine, but I would encourage you to read through the book project-by-project and familiarize yourself with all of the skills.

A Note About the Cover Painting

I created the composition on the cover using elements from the projects in this book. If you wish to paint a similar design, trace and cut out individual pattern elements and arrange them until you're happy with the composition. Then refer to the projects for instructions on painting each element.

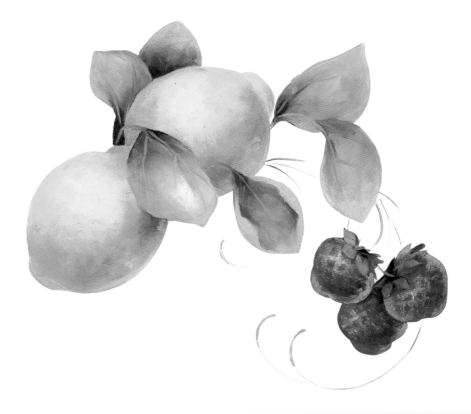

Materials

WATER MIXABLE OILS

Rich colors and ease of blending have attracted artists to oil paints for centuries. In today's society, we are much more health conscious and environmentally aware than the artists that came before us. Many painters today don't want to try traditional oil paints because of the potential health hazards of the solvents used in thinning and cleaning up the paint.

If you find yourself reluctant to use oils for this reason, but have always admired their glowing richness, try the new Artisan Water Mixable Oil Colors by Winsor & Newton.

What is so appealing about these paints is that you can clean your brushes with soap and water instead of solvents.

I use no mediums in my painting process, but if you want to use a glazing technique, you can use the mediums that Winsor & Newton makes specifically for water mixable paints. This eliminates the need for blending mediums that can cause health problems.

It is important to understand, however, that the term water mixable does not mean these paints can be thinned indefinitely with water. Manufacturers emphasize that these paints aren't designed to be thinned to a wash consistency, as you might do with acrylics or watercolors. Adding too much water may "underbind" the paint, which keeps it from adhering properly to the surface and diminishes its durability.

To thin the paint for linework or flecking techniques, it is preferable to use odorless turpenoid.

If you have questions regarding water mixable oil paints, contact Winsor & Newton at:

Winsor & Newton/ColArt
  Americans
P.O. Box 1396
Piscataway, NJ 08855-1396
Phone (732) 562-0770
www.winsornewton.com

My Basic Palette

- Titanium White
- Ivory Black
- Lemon Yellow (or Cadmium Lemon if using traditional oils)
- Cadmium Orange Hue
- Yellow Ochre
- Raw Sienna
- Burnt Umber
- Cadmium Red Light (or Cadmium Scarlet if using traditional oils)
- Permanent Alizarin Crimson
- Prussian Blue
- Cadmium Green Pale (only available in traditional oil)
- Oxide of Chromium (only available in traditional oil)

⚜HINT⚜ *Most oil paint color names are consistent between brands; however, there are a few exceptions. If you are using a brand other than Winsor & Newton, make sure you check the color against the color samples in each project and use a color that matches as closely as possible.*

Winsor & Newton Artists' Oil Colors	Other Brands
Cadmium Lemon	*Cadmium Yellow Light*
Cadmium Scarlet	*Cadmium Red Light*
Winsor Violet	*Dioxazine Purple*
Cadmium Green Pale	*Thalo Yellow Green*
Oxide of Chromium	*Chromium Oxide Green*

BASIC SUPPLIES

- Paper towels.
- Winsor & Newton series no. 710 brushes. These are sable chisel blenders that have a good spring to them and come to a sharp chisel edge. You will need sizes 2, 4, 6, 8 and 10. Don't try to save money by buying cheaper brushes; you'll find that a good brush is worth its weight in gold.
- A no. 1 round sable liner brush for scrollwork and detailing.
- Tracing paper.
- Graphite paper for transferring the design. You will need a white sheet for dark-colored backgrounds and a dark sheet for light-colored backgrounds.

- Odorless turpenoid for linework and flecking (and cleanup if you are using traditional oils).
- Brush cleaning jar with wire inside for odorless turpenoid.
- Bar of soap for cleanup if you are using water mixable oils.
- Lard oil for conditioning your brushes.
- Kneaded rubber eraser for erasing smudges or graphite lines.
- Delta Ceramcoat Red Iron Oxide acrylic. I use this as a basecoat under gold leaf.
- Gold leaf adhesive.
- Gold leaf sealer.
- Gold leaf sheets. These come in small packs of twenty-five sheets.
- Bristle brush for applying gold leaf adhesive.

- Lintless, soft cloth for rouging and antiquing. An old T-shirt works well.
- Piece of velvet or pantyhose to buff the gold leaf.
- Krylon Matte Finish spray no. 1311 for force drying the oils (optional).
- Krylon Indoor/Outdoor Varnish Spray, Clear Wood Finish no. 1701 for the final varnish.
- Brush Up! This product is terrific for cleaning dried oil paints out of brushes.
- Winsor & Newton Artgel. This is great for cleaning hands or as a spot treatment for clothes.
- 9" × 12" (22.9cm × 30.5cm) canvas boards. I use these as supports for my palette. I paint them the color of my background and cover them with wax paper.
- Wax paper.

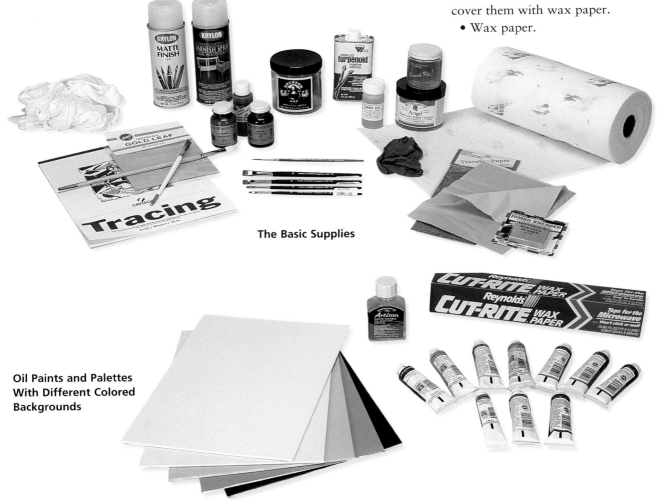

The Basic Supplies

Oil Paints and Palettes With Different Colored Backgrounds

SUPPLIES FOR BACK-GROUND PREPARATION

For acrylic backgrounds you will need:

• 250- and 400-grit wet/dry sandpaper.

• Tack cloth for removing dust after sanding.

• Scotch Brand blue tape. This is a low-tack tape that won't leave any residue behind. Use this for creating sharp edges between background colors. It can be found at any hardware store.

• Plastic wrap to create modeled backgrounds.

• Delta Ceramcoat acrylic paints (see color swatches at right for the projects in this book).

• Jo Sonja's All Purpose Sealer. Mix this sealer with your acrylic background color for a one step seal and basecoat.

• Sponge brushes in 1 inch (2.5cm) and 2 inch (5.1cm) widths.

• Krylon Matte Finish spray no. 1311. This acrylic spray will seal acrylic backgrounds.

DELTA CERAMCOAT ACRYLIC PAINTS

Blue Danube
02013

Lavender Lace
02016

Black Cherry
02484

Dresden Flesh
02033

Raw Linen
02546

Red Iron Oxide
02020

Old Parchment
02092

Wedgwood Green
02070

Black
02506

Sandstone
02402

White
02505

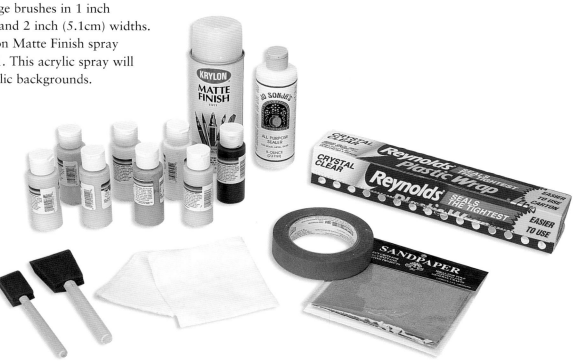

Supplies for Preparing Your Backgrounds

BRUSH CARE

Your painting can only be as good as your tools. If you are trying to paint with worn-out brushes, you'll find yourself struggling and becoming discouraged.

My brushes can last a year or more, and I paint frequently. I attribute the life of my brushes to the way I use my brush on the palette and project and to the care that I give them when I am through painting.

Don't try to get away with using the same brushes for oils and acrylics. Have a different set for each medium.

Sable brushes are made of real animal hair. Shampooing your own hair can strip it of its natural oils, so you use conditioners. It's just as important to use conditioners on your painting brushes to prevent the hair from drying out and breaking.

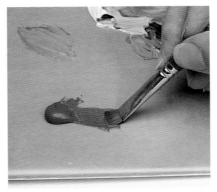

Loading Your Brush
When loading your brush on the palette, hold the brush at a 45° angle and always pull the brush toward you so that the bristles aren't being stressed.

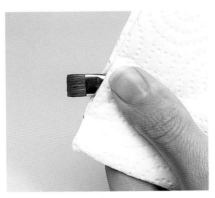

Wiping Your Brush
When drywiping your brush, pinch the brush between the folds of a paper towel and pull the brush toward you.

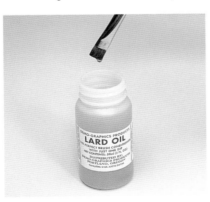

Conditioning Your Brush
When you're done painting, rinse your brush in water (for water-soluble paints) or odorless turpenoid (for traditional oils). After rinsing thoroughly, dip your brush in lard oil to condition it. If any paint is left in the ferrule of the brush, the conditioner will keep it soft until the next time you clean your brush.

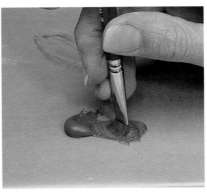

What's Wrong With This Picture?
Holding the brush at this angle and pressing down will only increase the stress on the hairs of the brush. This will quickly break the hairs and ruin your brush.

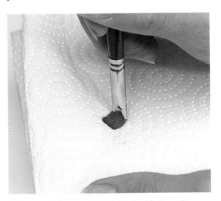

What's Wrong With This Picture?
Patting your brush on a paper towel in an up-and-down motion will quickly break the hairs on your brush.

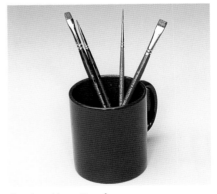

Storing Your Brushes
Store your brushes with the hairs facing up so that the lard oil can run down into the ferrule and the bristles aren't bent out of shape. When you're ready to paint again, just wipe the brush in a paper towel.

CHAPTER TWO

Preparing and Finishing the Surface

ACRYLIC BACKGROUND

Backgrounds play a very important role in the painting process. If the surface has not been properly prepared, you may find yourself struggling with a variety of problems.

An unsealed surface can cause the paint to bleed or soak in so rapidly that you can't blend.

Too much sanding can cause the surface to be too slick for the paint to adhere to properly.

It's not brain surgery, but it helps to read and follow all background preparation instructions carefully to avoid any problems.

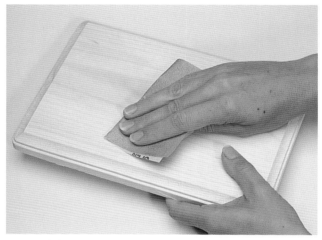

1 Sand the wood with 250-grit sandpaper. Always sand with the grain.

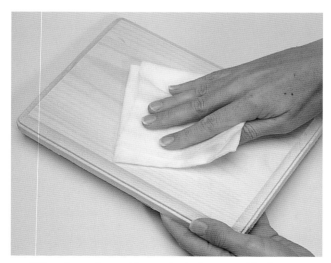

2 Wipe the surface with a tack cloth to get rid of any wood particles.

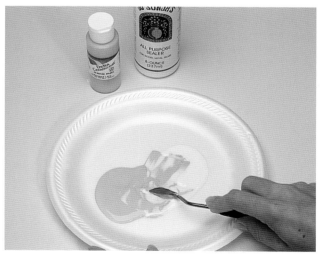

3 Mix one part of the acrylic basecoat color with one part Jo Sonja's All Purpose Sealer. This will seal and basecoat the surface in one step.

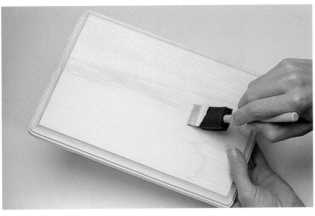

4 Apply a thin coat of the basecoat mixture using a sponge brush. Let dry, then lightly sand with 400-grit sandpaper. Wipe again with a tack cloth.

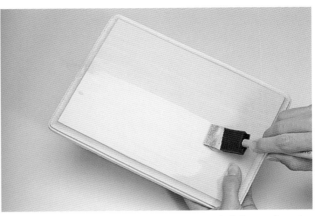

5 Apply a second basecoat. If necessary, lightly sand again. Don't make the surface too smooth; you want the surface to have some tooth so the paint will adhere.

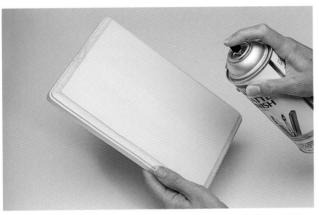

6 When the acrylic basecoat has dried, spray lightly with Krylon Matte Finish spray no. 1311.

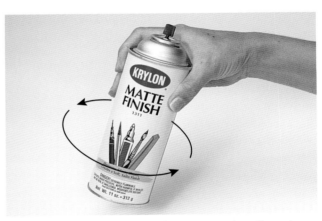

7 Before spray drying, twirl the can around until you hear the ball inside move freely.

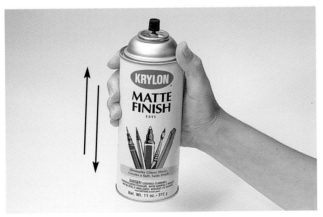

8 Next, shake the can up and down.

What's Wrong With This Picture?
The can is too close to the surface and has been left in one spot too long, creating drips. Always move the can back and forth, never stopping in one spot.

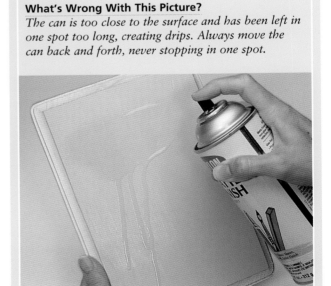

TRANSFERRING THE DESIGN

When I started decorative painting, my younger brother didn't feel that I was an artist because I was using someone else's pattern and not drawing the design freehand. In his eyes, I was copying, and copying is not art.

This always bothered me because I felt I was an artist. When a musician plays someone else's music, he or she is still a musician. When a seamstress sews a dress from a pattern, she is still a seamstress.

Starting from a pattern does not diminish the fact that we are artists. Use whatever means necessary to make a painting convey the illusion of realism.

My decorative art background has taught me so much about painting—how to blend, an understanding of color and the relationships of one color to another, and many more aspects that will be explained in this book. Whether you are a weekend hobbyist or a serious artist, decorative painting can be an important part of your learning process.

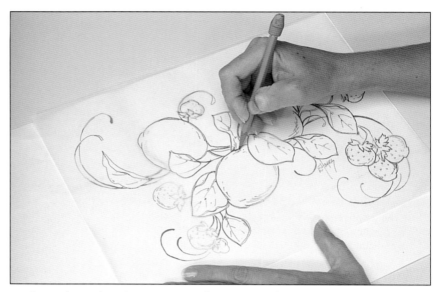

1 Lay a sheet of tracing paper over the pattern and trace the outlines of the elements with a pencil or ballpoint pen. Don't trace any details, such as veins or linework.

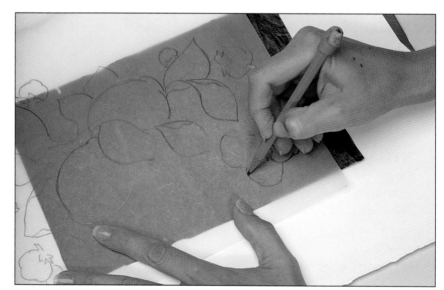

2 Position the tracing on the project. It's helpful to tape the tracing paper down so it doesn't slide around. Lay a piece of graphite paper underneath. Begin tracing the pattern using light pressure. Pressing too hard can indent the wood.

&**HINT**& *I would recommend that you don't become a slave to the pattern. Flowers and leaves are constantly changing in their environment as the wind blows and as they grow. Don't be afraid to change a leaf shape or add a flower if it will make the design fit your surface better.*

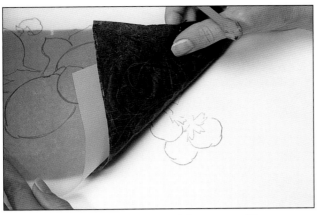

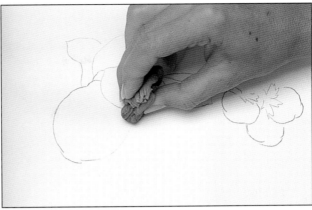

3 After tracing a small section of the pattern, lift a corner of the graphite paper to check that the graphite lines are coming through. I've managed to trace an entire pattern before realizing I had the graphite paper upside down.

4 After you have traced the pattern onto your surface, take a kneaded eraser and erase any smudges and lighten any pattern lines that are too dark.

VARNISHING

Varnishing your painting serves two purposes. First, it helps protect the painting from dust and dirt that can accumulate on the surface over time. Second, it brings out the richness of color in the oil paints. As paint dries it tends to dull down. Varnishing brings back the life in your painting.

I prefer a satin varnish over a gloss varnish, but this is purely personal. I've never had much success with brush-on varnishes, so I've stayed with the spray-on varnishes.

Giving your piece several light coats—and sanding between coats—will give you the best results. Always spray outside.

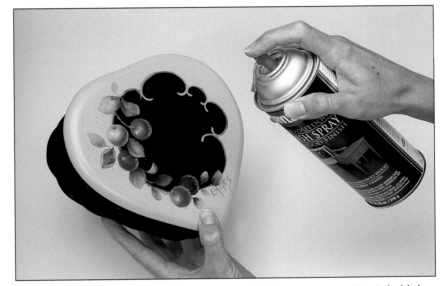

Use the same method to apply varnish as you did the matte spray: Don't hold the can too close to the surface, or spray one area too long.

CHAPTER THREE

Knowing Your Palette

THE PALETTE

I am always amazed at the palettes I see students using when I teach my classes—paper plates and waxed trays from grocery stores are just a few. These types of palettes don't give you enough room to brush mix the colors or place the paints on the palette in an orderly fashion. In addition, if you use a palette that isn't impervious to oils and tends to soak up the linseed oil in the paint, you'll find yourself struggling with paint that is too dry and tends to ball up on you.

I use a 9" × 12" (22.9cm × 30.5cm) canvas board that I paint the same color as my project background. After basecoating the board, I cover it with wax paper which I tape on from the back. I keep several of these on hand and use them over and over again. This size of palette gives me plenty of room for blending and mixing.

For years I used a white disposable palette. When I was working on a medium to dark background, the colors that I mixed and thought were the right colors on my white palette wouldn't look the same on my dark background. I found myself struggling to mix the right color on a cool white palette whenever I was painting on any color that wasn't white. That's why basecoating the palette with the background color is so important. I can tell immediately on my palette whether the color is too light or too dark, too warm or too cool. The less guessing and struggling I have to do when mixing colors and judging values, the more my confidence builds.

Setting Up Your Palette

This is how I set up my palette. Yellow goes in the top left-hand corner. The colors to the right follow the color wheel: yellows, oranges and reds. Going down the right-hand side of the palette there are violets, blues and greens. The black, yellow and white across the bottom are the colors I use to create greens for leaves. Going up the left-hand side I place my earth yellows starting with the darkest, dullest yellow, which is Burnt Umber, and continuing up the line with cleaner, brighter yellows. I place white in the center for highlights.

Although I may not use every color pictured here in each project, I always place the colors in the same order.

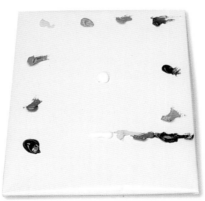

General Palette Set Up for Light-Colored Backgrounds

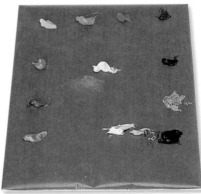

General Palette Set Up For Dark-Colored Backgrounds

USING ACRYLICS INSTEAD OF OILS

If you prefer to paint in acrylics, I recommend you use Winsor & Newton Finity Artists' Acrylic Colors. Their pigments are comparable to the oil colors and they remain workable slightly longer than other acrylic colors. The acrylic equivalents of the basic oil palette are shown at right.

If you prefer to use another brand of acrylics, Tru-Color Systems has a wonderful color conversion book that includes oil and acrylic conversions. It can be ordered through Tru-Color Systems, Inc., P.O. Box 486, Danville, Indiana 46122. Phone (317) 745-7535, fax (317) 745-1886 or E-mail *comments@gotcs.com.* You can visit their Web site at www.gotcs.com.

When working in acrylics, I find that I need more workable time than the paints allow, so I use an acrylic retarder to extend the drying time. Otherwise my techniques are the same as for oils.

First basecoat and let that stage dry, then rewet your surface with the basecoat plus a little retarder and begin shading and highlighting. Blend by using short, choppy strokes between colors.

You may have to continually pick up paint on your brush to keep a wet surface while blending, and you may need to work a little faster than you would with oils.

FINITY ARTISTS' ACRYLIC COLORS

 Ivory Black

 Cadmium Yellow Light (substitute for Lemon Yellow)

 Yellow Ochre

 Raw Sienna

 Burnt Umber

 Cadmium Red Light

 Cadmium Orange

 Permanent Alizarin Crimson

 Indanthrene Blue (substitute for Prussian Blue)

 Chromium Oxide Green

 Cadmium Green Pale (mix Indanthrene Blue + Cadmium Yellow Light + Titanium White)

 Titanium White

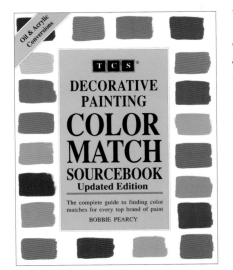

HINT *Have you ever wondered why the keys on a typewriter are always placed in the same order with each model made? Would it be possible to play the piano if every manufacturer were to place the keys in a different order? The answer is obvious. An artist must also develop a pattern when setting out his or her palette and continue to use that same pattern throughout the painting process. Painting is hard enough without having to guess where the colors are on your palette. If you don't use my method, create a method that makes sense to you and stick to it.*

CHAPTER FOUR

Brush Mixing and Blending

Brush mixing produces subtle differences in value and color that can't be achieved through palette knife mixing. There is a tendency to overmix the colors when palette knife mixing, killing their vibrancy. It's like leaving the blender on too long and ending up with mush.

Since I use very little paint, I can brush mix exactly what I need and there is little waste. When you use a palette knife, you mix more than you need and therefore waste a lot of paint.

While painting I may find that I want a slightly darker or lighter version of the color I'm using, or I may need a slightly warmer or cooler version. By brush mixing I can gradually add paint to achieve the value, color and temperature I'm looking for. I am continually reinforcing my mixes while painting by pulling color from the main puddle into the loading area.

⊰HINT ⊱ With each project I've included color swatches with the mixes listed. While I can give you basic color swatches for the base, shade and highlight mixes, I couldn't possibly give you a color swatch for every color that I use. Each time I brush mix the base into the shade area I'm creating another mix. When the highlight mix starts to blend into the base mix I'm creating yet another color. When a tint is added and blended in it creates another subtle change. This is what is so beautiful about brush mixing.

Brush Mixing Step-by-Step

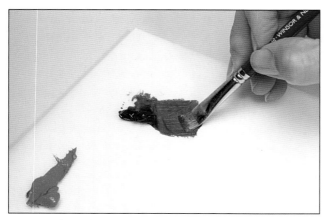

1 Begin by pulling the color away from the main puddle to create a loading area. For this demonstration I've started with Permanent Alizarin Crimson.

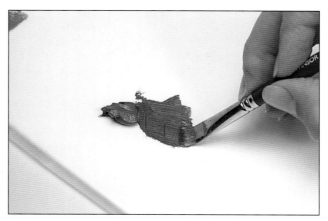

2 Without wiping your brush, begin to pull some of the second color, Raw Sienna in this case, away from the main puddle. You've now mixed a loading area of Permanent Alizarin Crimson plus Raw Sienna.

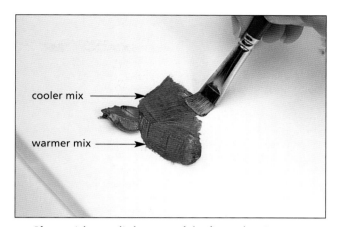

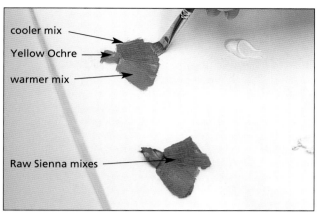

3 If you pick up a little more of the first color, Permanent Alizarin Crimson, and begin mixing it just to the right of the previous mixture, you'll have two loading areas by this one puddle of Raw Sienna. The first loading area has more Raw Sienna in it so it is warmer, while the other loading area has more Permanent Alizarin Crimson in it so it is cooler. You now have a warm and cool version of the same color.

4 Next, move up to Yellow Ochre and mix Permanent Alizarin Crimson into it just as you did with the Raw Sienna. You're basically mixing the same color families as you did when using Raw Sienna, but they are a little lighter and purer with Yellow Ochre. Once again, you have a warm and cool version of the mix.

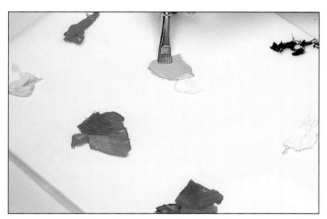

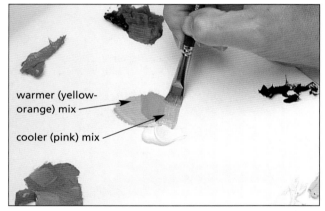

5 By mixing the color on your brush with Titanium White in a new loading area, you can begin to see whether you have more yellow or more Permanent Alizarin Crimson in your mix. Here it's obvious that my brush had more yellow tones in it when I began mixing into white because the color leans more toward yellow-orange than red.

6 If you pick up a little more Permanent Alizarin Crimson on your brush and begin mixing into the white, you can create a pinker or cooler version of the first mix. Notice that I don't eliminate the first mixture, but move over to create another loading area. I want to create several loading areas around the puddle of color.

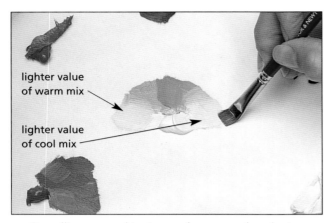

lighter value
of warm mix

lighter value
of cool mix

7 By pulling more white into each warm and cool mix you can create a lighter value of each mixture.

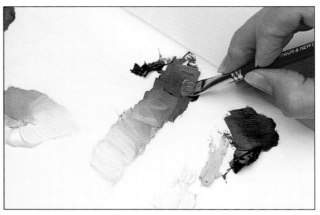

8 Here I'm creating a ribbon of values by mixing Prussian Blue and Ivory Black with more and more Titanium White. Within this ribbon of blue I have several values I can choose from.

Leaf Colors

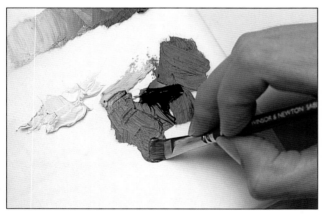

1 To mix greens for leaves, create a ribbon of color by mixing Ivory Black and Lemon Yellow, creating a dark olive green. Black and yellow create green because Ivory Black has a bluish tone and blue and yellow make green.

2 Continue to move over to the left and pull down more white into your mixes. As you mix white into this mix you will be able to tell whether you have more yellow or more black in your mix by the temperature. If you achieve a very grayed green, you have more black in your mix. If you end up with a very yellowish green, you have more yellow in the mix. At this stage, you want to mix a middle temperature green—not too hot and not too cold. Continue mixing until you have a ribbon of green mixtures from dark to light.

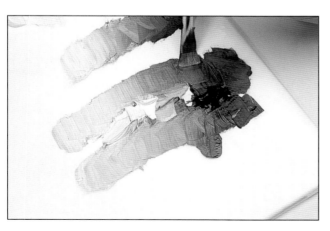

3 Since you want warms and cools within your leaves, also mix a cooler version of the green ribbon by adding less yellow to the first mixture.

Warm and Cool

I use the terms "warm" and "cool" a lot. They refer to the temperature of the color being used. There are six colors on the color wheel—three warm and three cool. Yellow, orange and red are warm colors and blue, green and violet are cool colors.

An easy way to remember this is to associate the colors with something. The sun is yellow and provides us with warmth. When a fire burns the coals turn orange and red. When we are cold our lips turn blue. See how easy this is?

Orange is the warmest color because it sits between two other warm colors. Blue is the coolest color because it sits between two other cool colors.

However, each color also has a warm and cool side, depending on which color family it leans toward. For example, red-orange is warmer than red-violet. Yellow-green is warmer than blue-green.

As I will explain many times throughout this book, the characteristic of a color greatly depends on what is surrounding it. If a warm green is placed on a warmer orange tone, the green will appear cool. If the same green is placed on a cool blue tone, it will appear warmer. Value and temperature are greatly influenced by their surroundings.

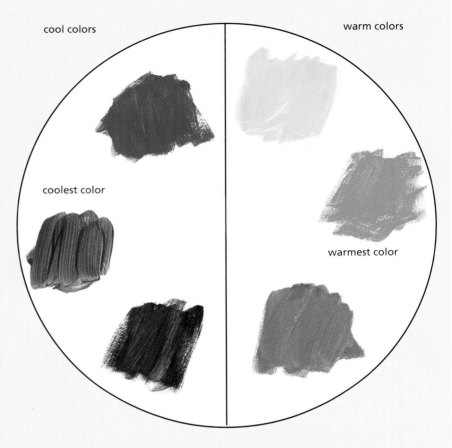

cool colors

warm colors

coolest color

warmest color

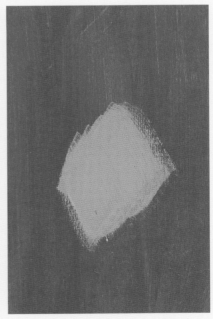

A warm color on a warm background looks cooler.

The same warm color on a cool background looks warmer.

Toning Down Colors

I prefer to start my paintings with rather dull colors and increase their intensity as I continue to refine. I find this much easier than dulling down a project that has become too intense.

The key to toning down a color is to dull down each object's base color with its complement, or mix a gray tone into the base color.

A strong accent color or tint is sometimes all that is needed to bring a painting to life.

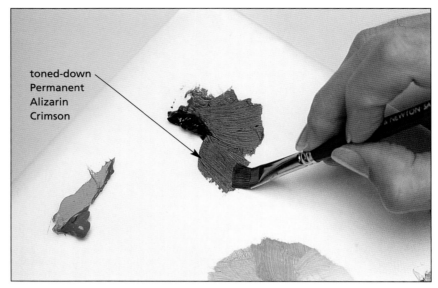

toned-down Permanent Alizarin Crimson

To tone down a color I use its equivalent-value complement. Here I've mixed some dark greens into my Permanent Alizarin Crimson.

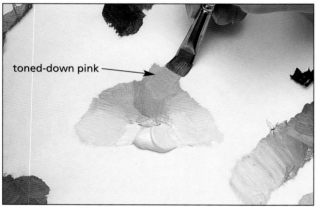

toned-down pink

To achieve a toned-down version of my light pink mixes I pick up a little light green—which is the pink mix's equivalent-value complement—and brush mix, creating another loading area. Around this puddle of paint I now have six different mixes from which to choose.

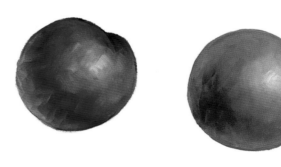

I painted the plum on the left using Prussian Blue plus Titanium White. Its color is very intense and harsh. To paint the plum on the right, I first made a gray mixture of Ivory Black and Titanium White, then added a little Prussian Blue. I then added warmer colors to the light area of the plum to balance the coldness of the blue. This plum is a lot easier to look at.

Choppy Blending

Choppy blending refers to the way in which I blend my colors together. I prefer a "painterly" look in which my brushstrokes are still evident rather than completely blended out to a photo realistic smoothness. Therefore I leave my brushstrokes a bit on the choppy side. This choppiness creates personality and vitality in your painting.

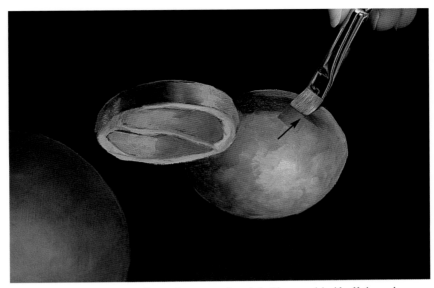

1 When blending two colors, place your brush half on and half off the color to be blended, in this case the shading on the orange, and begin to pull at a diagonal.

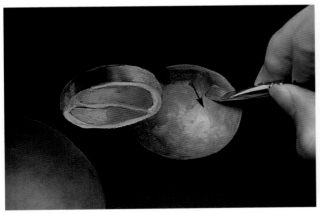

2 Next, pull your brush through the color going in the opposite direction. Imagine you're creating Xs between the colors, pulling one color into the other. My brush is constantly moving back and forth when I blend.

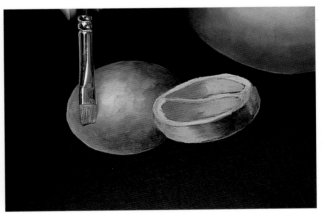

3 Continue to move your brush back and forth between the colors. Dry wipe your brush anytime you feel that you've picked up a lot of paint on your brush. Refine the blending until you are happy. I prefer to see a slight modeling of the color instead of a smoothly blended surface. This gives the illusion of texture and life.

CHAPTER FIVE

Painting Leaves

Somehow painting leaves was always overlooked when I was taking classes. There was never enough time to properly teach how to paint leaves and their importance to a design.

When I teach, I constantly hear moans and groans when it comes time to do the leaves. But I always enjoyed leaves. For me they represent the supporting actors that make the star look so good.

Value and temperature are critical to the development of realistic leaves. The most common mistake I see students make is allowing the leaves to become too warm and too intense for the rest of the design. This makes them "pop out" so they are the very first thing you see.

⊰ H I N T ⊱ *The key to painting leaves is realizing their importance to a design and not giving them so much attention that they outshine the main elements. Leaves need to relate in color, value and temperature to the main element of the design.*

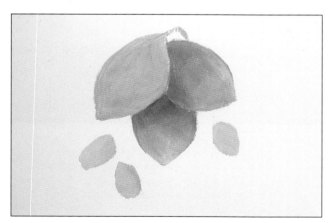

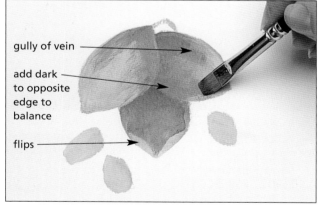

gully of vein

add dark to opposite edge to balance

flips

1 Using the values from your ribbon of greens (see page 18) begin basing in the leaves, concentrating on keeping the top leaf warmer and lighter and the bottom leaves a little darker and cooler. Since I'm painting on a light background, I paint the little filler leaves in a light value green.

2 Since I have three values of leaves in this cluster, I will need three shading colors—one appropriate for each of the three leaves. Pick up a darker value green than the base color of each leaf and start placing this shading color in the most obvious dark areas. Pull this color out to form the gully of the vein area. Balance this shade by adding some dark to the other side of each leaf; this color should be thin and fuzzy. On the darkest bottom leaf I've placed the shade to form flips.

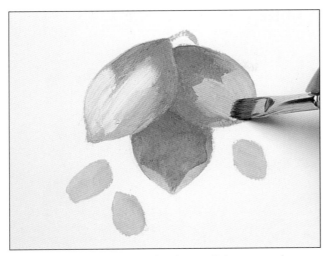

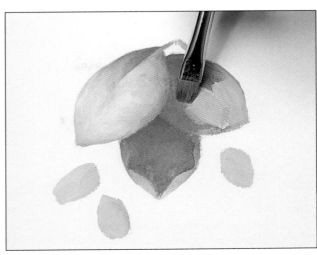

3 Dry wipe your brush and pick up a lighter green from the ribbon of values. Place this color in the most obvious light area. Repeat for each of the three leaves, using a lighter value appropriate to that leaf. Notice I place light on both sides of the leaves; I'm always trying to balance my darks and lights. Since I'm working with lighter colors, the paint needs to be thicker to make it more opaque.

4 Dry wipe your brush and place it half on and half off the highlight color you just applied. Start to blend where the two colors meet using short, choppy strokes. My brush is constantly moving in a criss-cross motion. Any time I feel I have a buildup of paint on my brush I will dry wipe it before I continue blending.

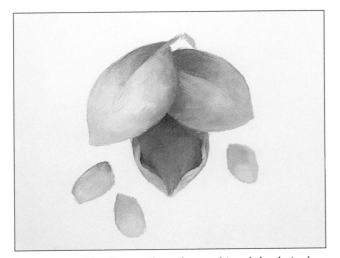

5 Continue blending until you have achieved the desired look. I concentrate on making the top leaf warm and light with a lot of detail. As the leaves continue down in planes, they get darker, cooler and less detailed.

What's Wrong With This Picture?
These leaves are too warm for the cool blue background and the blue plums they surround. Notice how the yellow-green jumps out at you, seeming to float above the plums?

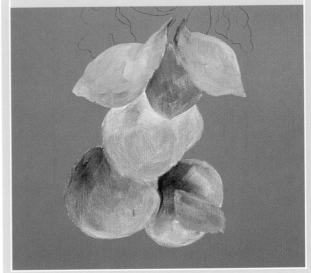

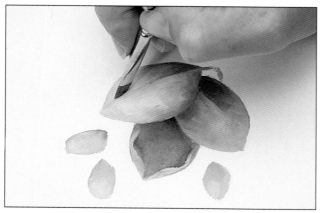

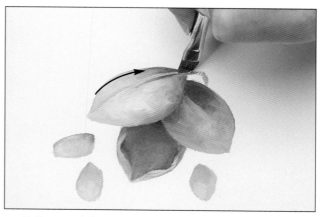

6 To create the suggestions of stems and veins, place a dry
wiped brush on its chisel and start at the tip of the leaf.

7 Pull toward the stem end of the leaf, keeping the chisel
on the dark side of the gully.

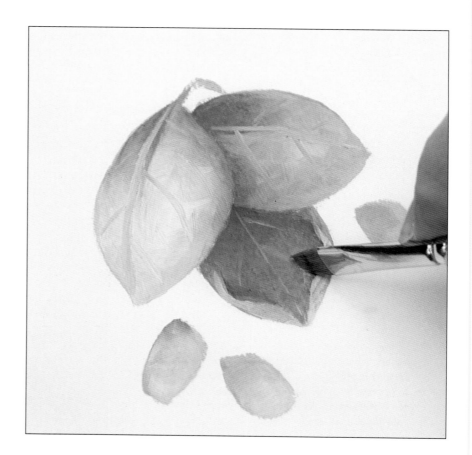

8 Pull side veins out from the main
vein following the gentle curve of
the leaf.

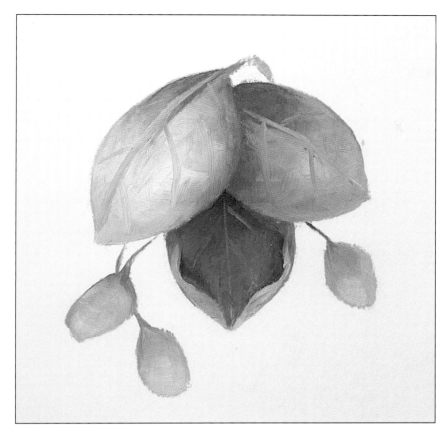

9 Add stems for the little filler leaves using a liner brush or the chisel end of your brush. Now stand back and analyze. You should have a nice balance of darks and lights and warms and cools, and a mingling of colors within your leaves that create life and personality.

What's Wrong With This Picture?
The dark on this top leaf has been pulled down too far toward the tip. Instead of balancing my darks and lights, I have a definite light and dark side. This cuts the leaf in half.

The veins are also too thick and dark. They are the first things I see in this leaf. Veins should be very light, almost more of a suggestion of a vein.

If your veins become too strong, gently brush over them with a dry wiped brush to soften them into the wet paint.

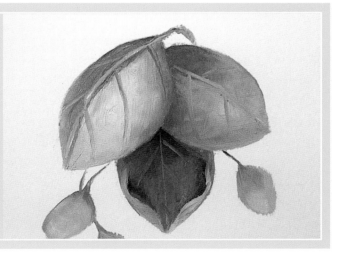

CHAPTER SIX

Step-By-Step Projects

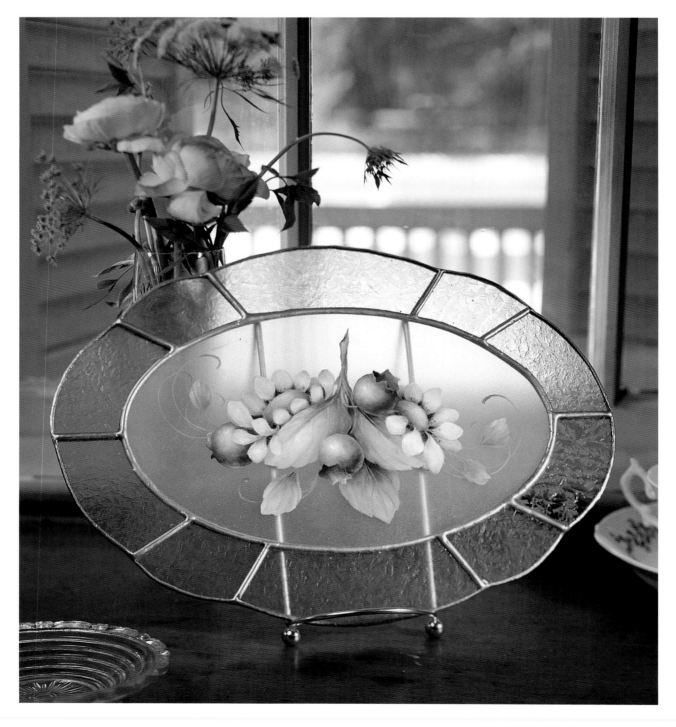

Blueberries and Daisies

START WITH THE FOCAL POINT

The scariest part about painting is the first brushstroke. Deciding where to start can be a dilemma. I always start with the focal point—the area that your eyes are drawn to first.

The focal point can be a single element of the design or a whole area. Determine what the focal point is on your project.

Next, think in planes. Generally I'll start with the topmost main element. On this blueberry piece there are two blueberries that are both on top. The lower blueberry is the focal point because it has more contrast surrounding it, thus drawing your eye toward it.

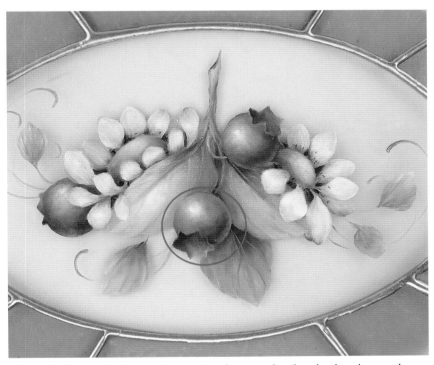

This is the focal point because it contains the most detail and value change, drawing your eye here first.

Preparing the Background

The wonderful thing about painting on glass is that no background preparation is needed. Lay your pattern under the glass and trace with a pencil.

Basing in the Design

Great endings start with simple beginnings. I simplify everything in the beginning stages just by concentrating on the correct base color and, more importantly, the correct value. I don't try to achieve any strong lights or darks yet. I save those for the detailing stage.

Use the biggest brush possible for the area you're working in. Don't try to paint a large apple

with a no. 4 brush. You'll never get done and it will ruin your brush.

If the brush feels too large, then it's probably just the right size. I've always loved oil painter Helen Van Wyk's saying, "Start with a broom and finish with a needle."

Spray Drying

After you've based in the entire design, spray dry using Krylon Matte Finish spray no. 1311.

After everything is based in, you can concentrate on shading and highlighting to create form and interest. As you do this, spray dry anytime you feel you can't get the desired detail. This will help you to achieve strong lights and darks

without overblending.

You might find it necessary to reapply a little base color after spray drying to help blend the highlight in. You don't need to basecoat the entire element as you did in the beginning; just brush a little more wet color into the light area to help with the blending.

HINT *Display this stained glass piece painted with blueberries and daisies on a small table easel or hang it from a gold chain in your window.*

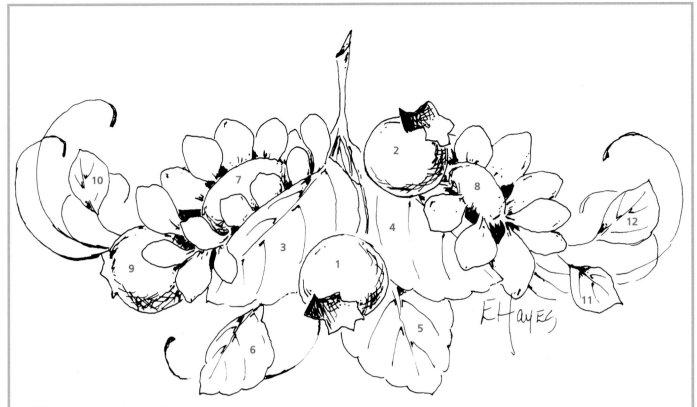

This pattern may be hand-traced or photocopied for personal use only. Enlarge 103% on a photocopier to return to full size. Each element is numbered according to its importance to the design. Start basing in with number one and continue in the order of importance.

⊰HINT ⊱ Spray drying with Krylon Matte Finish spray no. 1311 is a great way to eliminate the drying time when painting with oils. The spray doesn't actually dry the paint, it puts a protective coating on top of the wet oil paint. You can paint over this dry surface immediately (see page 11 for spraying instructions).

The key to spray drying is using thin layers of paint and spray drying within a few hours of ending your painting session. As time passes, the oil paints will start to dry at different rates. If you wait until the next day to spray dry, the oils will be in different stages of drying and the spray will create wrinkling or crazing in your painting.

So remember:
- *Use thin layers of paint.*
- *Several light coats of spray are better than one heavy coat.*
- *Always spray at the end of the painting session.*
- *Most importantly, always spray outside and let your piece dry before bringing it inside.*

Materials List

COLOR MIXES

BLUEBERRIES

Base
Titanium White
+ Ivory Black +
Prussian Blue

Shade
Ivory Black +
Prussian Blue

Accent
Permanent
Alizarin Crimson

Highlight
Base +
Titanium White

Reflected Light
Ivory Black + Titanium
White + a touch of cool
leaf highlight color

DAISIES

Base
Titanium White
+ Yellow Ochre
+ Ivory Black

Shade
Permanent
Alizarin Crimson
+ Ivory Black

Highlight
Base + more
Titanium White

Tint
Titanium White
+ a little
Ivory Black +
Prussian Blue

DAISY CENTERS

Base
Yellow Ochre +
Lemon Yellow

Shade
Permanent
Alizarin Crimson
+ Raw Sienna

Highlight
Lemon Yellow +
Titanium White

WARM LEAVES

Base
Ivory Black +
Lemon Yellow +
Titanium White

Shade
Base + Ivory
Black

Highlight
Base + a little
Lemon Yellow +
Titanium White

COOL LEAVES

Base
same as warm
leaves but
use less Lemon
Yellow

Shade
same as warm
leaves but
use less Lemon
Yellow

Highlight
same as warm
leaves but
use less Lemon
Yellow

SURFACE

This stained glass oval can be purchased from Cooper's Works, 1360 Berryman Avenue, Library, PA 15129. Phone (412) 831-0999.

WINSOR & NEWTON ARTISAN WATER MIXABLE OILS

- Lemon Yellow
- Yellow Ochre
- Raw Sienna
- Permanent Alizarin Crimson
- Ivory Black
- Titanium White
- Prussian Blue

BRUSHES

- no. 2, no. 4 and no. 6 sable chisel blenders
- no. 1 round sable liner

ADDITIONAL SUPPLIES

- pencil
- Krylon Matte Finish spray no. 1311
- oil palette
- paper towels
- odorless turpenoid

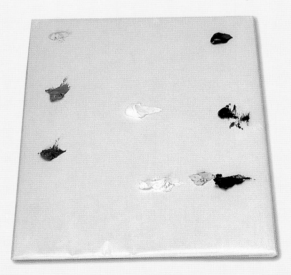

Since there is no basecoat color for this glass piece, basecoat your palette board with a light color.

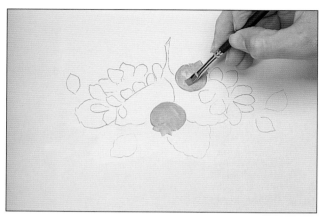

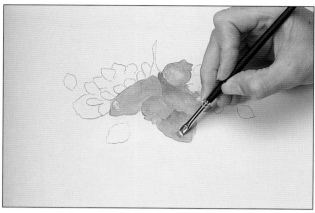

1 Base in the top two blueberries with Titanium White plus Ivory Black plus a little Prussian Blue.

2 Working down in planes, base in the leaves with Ivory Black plus Lemon Yellow plus Titanium White. Concentrate on basing the top leaf in a warmer, lighter tone and the bottom leaves in darker and cooler tones. Don't paint in paint-by-number fashion around the daisy petals that are peeking over the leaves. Instead, fuzz the leaf color into these petals. The petals can be reestablished when you base in the daisy.

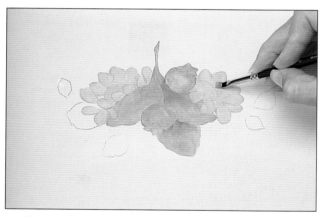

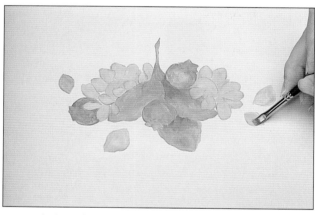

3 Base in the daisy petals with Titanium White plus Yellow Ochre plus Ivory Black. Base in the center of the daisy with Yellow Ochre plus Lemon Yellow.

4 With the colors from steps one and two, base in the far left blueberry and the little filler leaves. Keep the little leaves light so that the focal point remains within the top blueberry area.

⁂ **HINT** ⁂ *Base, shade, highlight—this is the correct order in which to develop your paintings. You've probably heard the saying "fat over lean." This principal applies to oil painting. After your basecoat is on, shade using the darker colors, keeping these colors thin and fuzzy. Save your highlighting for last because white is the most opaque and thickest paint on the palette.*

⁂ **HINT** ⁂ *When placing color on, use pressure on the brush to pull the color out onto your surface. When blending, move back on the handle and use little pressure.*

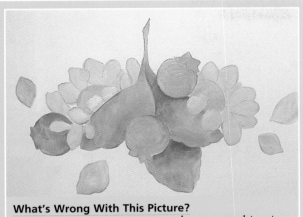

What's Wrong With This Picture?
It's very common to want to base everything in so that each color and element is very distinct and clear, as shown here. However, these distinct separations cause the painting to look stiff and are very hard on the eyes.

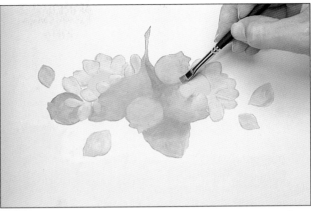

5 To eliminate hard edges after basing in the design, take a dry wiped brush and softly blend all the elements together. You shouldn't blend the elements completely; you are just creating a slightly "out-of-focus" look by softening and eliminating all hard edges. This technique serves two purposes: It eliminates that "paint-by-number" look and it starts to pull the elements together by adding tints. By blending the blueberry and leaf slightly together, you're working blue into the leaf and green into the blueberry, thus helping the two elements relate to one another. When everything has been based in and softened, spray dry with Krylon Matte Finish spray no. 1311, following the directions on page 11 and in the next step.

HINT ⌘ *After basing in each element, softly blend the elements together to get rid of any hard or strong lines. This is what I call the "out-of-focus" stage. Think of a camera with a manual focus: As you adjust the lens, everything gradually comes into focus. This is how your paintings should develop. As you detail the painting in later steps, you will create hard or found lines and bring your painting into focus.*

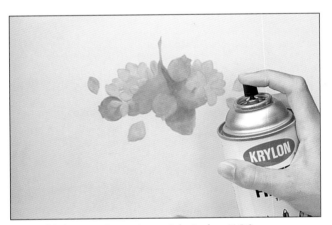

6 Hold the can about six to eight inches (15.2cm to 20.3cm) away from your surface. Hold your surface at a 45° angle. Always start spraying off into the air, then move the can onto your surface. Move back and forth, never stopping in one spot. Three light coats are better than one heavy coat. Let dry between coats and always spray outside.

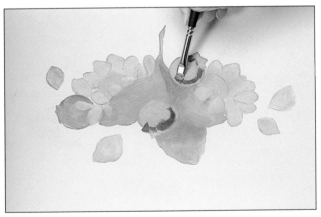

7 Now that the basecoat is dry, you can start detailing. Place a crescent-shaped shade on the blueberries with Ivory Black + Prussian Blue.

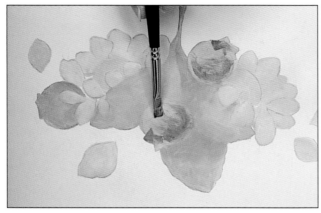

8 Fuzz this color out into the berry, keeping the strongest color within the crescent area.

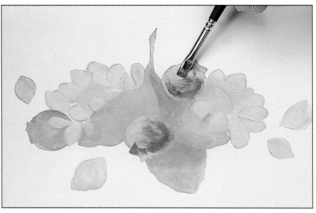

9 Place an accent color in the middle value area with Permanent Alizarin Crimson.

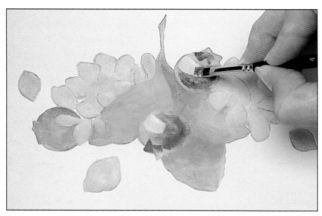

10 Place a highlight going across the blueberry with the base color plus more Titanium White.

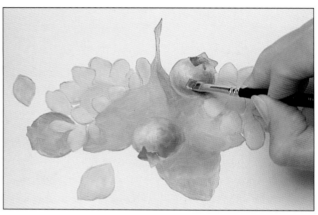

11 Place the brush where the two colors meet and blend the highlight out.

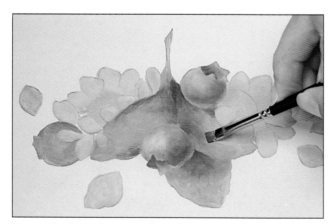

12 Shade the leaves with the base color plus more Ivory Black. Fuzz this color out into the middle value area.

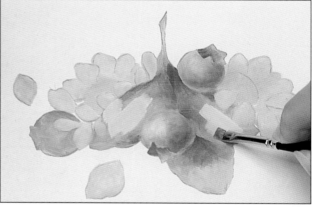

13 Place a highlight on the leaves with the leaf base color plus more Titanium White plus a little Lemon Yellow.

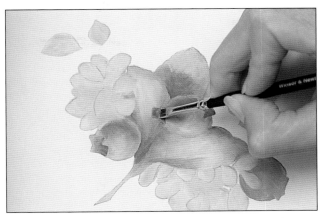

14 Start to blend where the two colors meet and blend out. If necessary, pick up a little base color to help blend.

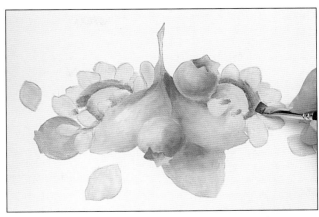

15 Shade the base of the petals on the daisy with Permanent Alizarin Crimson and Ivory Black. Place some of this color on the center for shading.

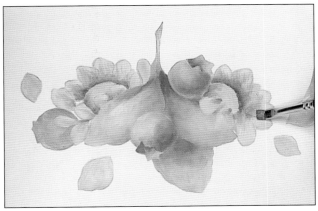

16 With a dry wiped brush, fuzz this color out into the petals, eliminating any hard edges.

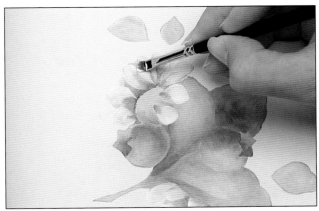

17 Place a parenthesis-shaped highlight on each petal with the base color plus a little Lemon Yellow plus Titanium White.

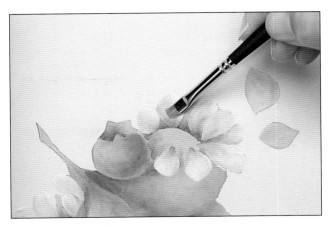

18 Blend the highlight on the petals, keeping the transition between the darks and lights soft. Concentrate on making the top petals lighter and warmer than the petals that are tucked behind.

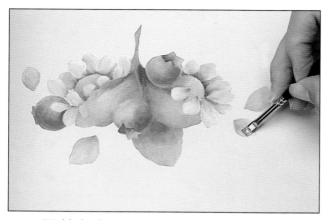

19 Highlight the centers with Lemon Yellow and Titanium White. Shade and refine the far left berry as you did the focal point berries. Shade and highlight the filler leaves, keeping them lighter and less detailed than the main leaves.

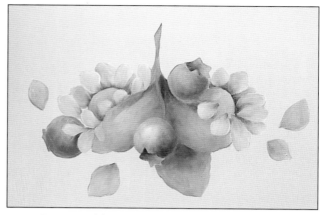

20 Now stand back and decide what else is needed. I placed a stronger highlight on my main berry with Titanium White, along with some stronger accents of Titanium White plus Prussian Blue.

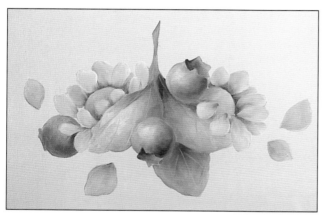

21 Adding stronger highlights and veins further refines the leaves. Refine the other berry with a stronger highlight.

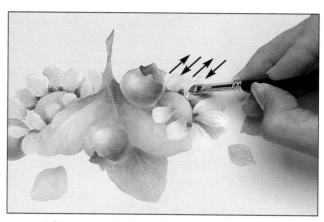

22 Add stronger darks to the base of the daisy petals and more highlights to the petals that come forward. Using the chisel edge of your brush, move back and forth on the petal to create suggestions of veins.

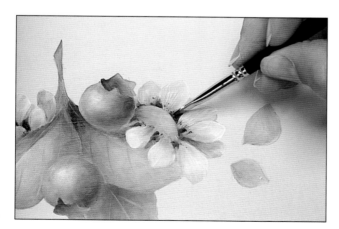

23 Place the pollen dots on with Ivory Black, using the corner of your brush. Twist the brush around with each dot so that they aren't uniform in appearance.

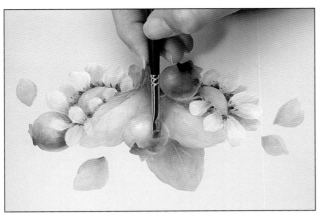

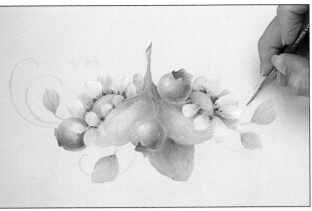

24 Place reflected light on the blueberries with Titanium White plus Ivory Black plus Prussian Blue. Blend out in a choppy fashion.

25 Thin some of the light greens on your palette down with odorless turpenoid. Using a liner brush and a loose hand, add linework. It will be easier if you always pull toward you. Work quickly to reduce shaky lines.

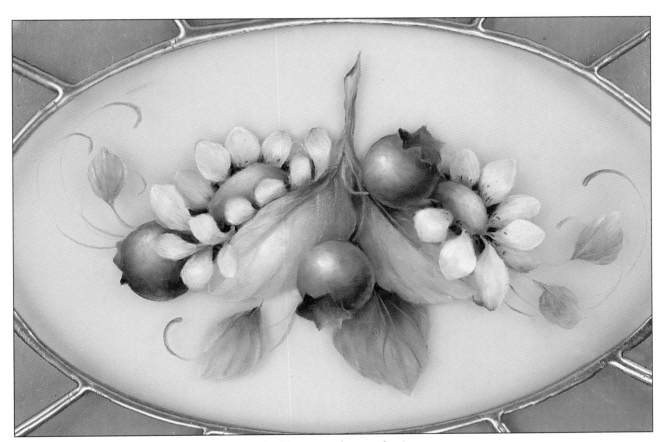

26 Shade the linework with darker greens and add accent colors on the tips with blues from the blueberries. Add blue tints to a few daisy petals to help them relate to the blueberries.

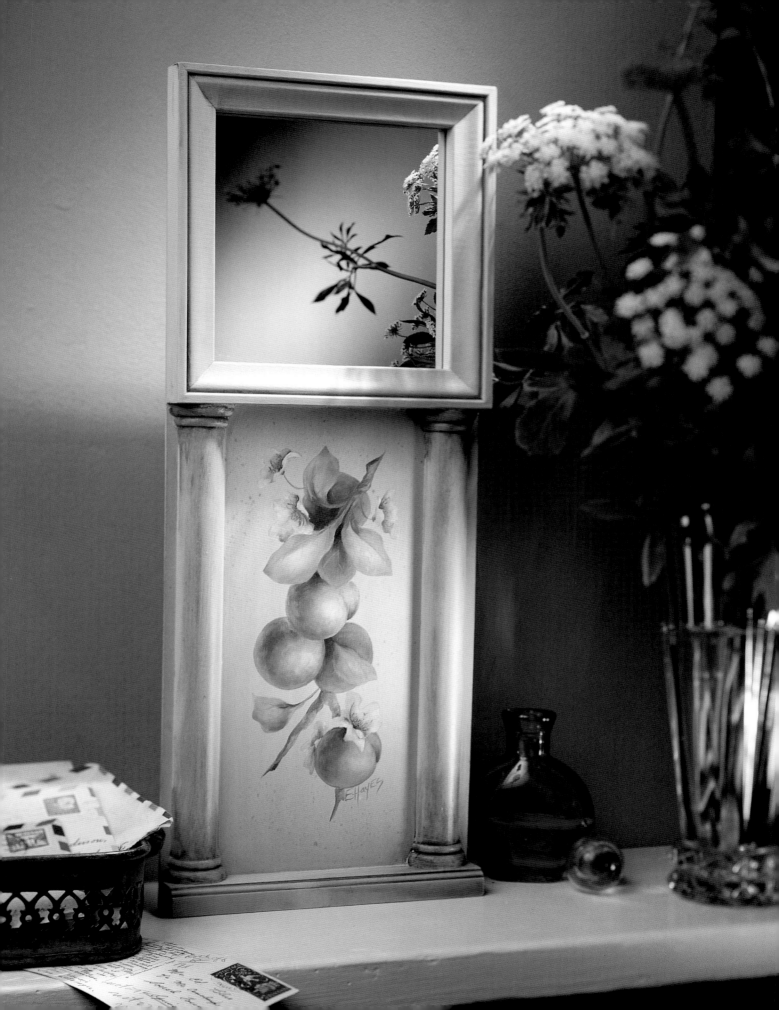

Plums and Blossoms

PAINTING IN CLUSTERS

The colors on this piece are very similar to the *Blueberries and Daisies* project. Instead of dealing with one mass of elements as you did in project one, you are dealing with three clusters.

When looking at this piece, your eye is drawn to the cluster of plums in the middle. This is the focal point, even though the plums aren't on the closest plane. The leaves are closer to you, but they are not the main element of the design.

Paint each cluster together as a unit. Always paint in order of importance to the design—start with the plums on the main cluster and continue painting each element going down in planes.

Continue with the other clusters in the same manner.

Preparing the Background

Basecoat the columned mirror following the preparation instructions found in chapter two. Use a half and half mix of Delta Ceramcoat Lavender Lace and White. Transfer the pattern.

This design is made up of three clusters. The focal point cluster is the plums in the middle. Instead of painting all of the plums, then all of the blossoms, etc., concentrate on painting each cluster as a whole. Start with the focal point cluster and paint every element within that cluster. Then base in every element in the top cluster, which is next in importance. Finish up with the bottom cluster.

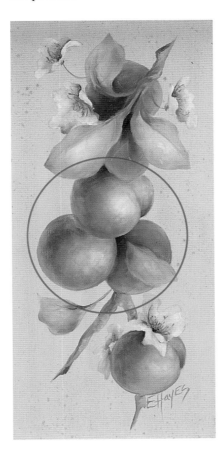

Materials List

SURFACE
This surface can be purchased through PCM Studios, 731 Highland Avenue, Suite D, Atlanta, GA 30312. Phone (404) 222-0348 or E-mail abjpcm@aol.com.

WINSOR & NEWTON ARTISAN WATER MIXABLE OILS
- Lemon Yellow
- Yellow Ochre
- Permanent Alizarin Crimson
- Ivory Black
- Titanium White
- Prussian Blue

BRUSHES
- no. 4, no. 6 and no. 8 sable chisel blenders
- no. 1 round sable liner

ADDITIONAL SUPPLIES
- Delta Ceramcoat Lavender Lace acrylic
- Delta Ceramcoat White acrylic
- 1-inch (2.5cm) sponge brush
- sandpaper
- Jo Sonja's All Purpose Sealer
- Krylon Matte Finish spray no. 1311
- odorless turpenoid
- paper towels
- disposable palette for oils
- dark graphite paper
- tracing paper
- ballpoint pen
- soft cloth
- Krylon Satin Varnish no. 1701

Materials List *continued*

COLOR MIXES

PLUMS

Base
Titanium White
+ Ivory Black +
Prussian Blue

Shade
Base +
Ivory Black +
Prussian Blue

Highlight
Base +
Titanium White

Tint
cool leaf
mixtures

BLOSSOMS

Base
Titanium White
+ Yellow Ochre
+ Ivory Black +
a little
Permanent
Alizarin Crimson

Shade
Base +
Ivory Black +
Permanent
Alizarin Crimson

Highlight
Base + a little
Lemon Yellow +
Titanium White

Tints
leaf mixtures

LEAVES
Add more
yellow for
warmer leaves,
less yellow for
cooler leaves.

Base
Ivory Black +
Lemon Yellow +
Titanium White

Shade
Base +
Ivory Black

Highlight
Base +
Titanium White

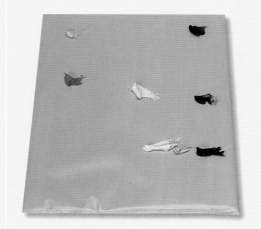

Base the palette board with the Lavender Lace/White acrylic mixture.

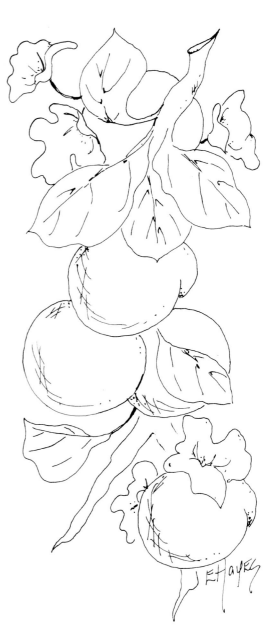

This pattern may be hand-traced or photocopied for personal use only. Enlarge 143% on a photocopier to return to full size.

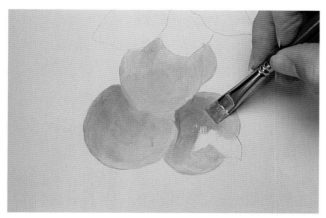

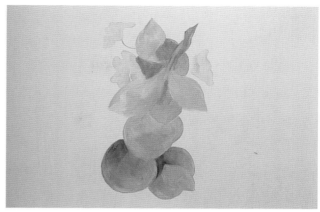

1 Working on the focal point cluster, base in the plums with Titanium White plus Ivory Black plus a little Prussian Blue. Concentrate on making the top plum lighter than the underneath plums. Don't try to paint around the little leaf; as you base in the bottom plum, fuzz some of the color into the leaf area. This will help eliminate hard edges where two elements meet.

2 Moving to the top cluster, base in the blossoms with a very light gray made from Titanium White plus a little Ivory Black plus a little Yellow Ochre plus a little Permanent Alizarin Crimson. Base in the third cluster in the same way. After everything is based in, soften all hard edges as explained on page 31. Erase any smudges with a kneaded eraser, then spray dry using Krylon Matte Finish spray no. 1311.

What's Wrong With This Picture?

The most common problem I see when teaching is that most students think if an element overlaps another element, the underneath element needs to be shaded all along the edge, as shown below. This causes a striped look. Positioning the shade colors in triangular overlaps will tell the viewer that an object is behind or in front of another.

Value change is also important in the shadowed areas; one shade mixture will not be adequate to shade every element in a design. Within a shadowed area I might have two to three values of shading; in the highlight area I might also have two to three values of highlight. Mix these in with your basecoat and tints and you have a recipe for a very good painting. "A pinch of this and a pinch of that and whatever else is in your cupboard," my grandmother would always say. Very sound advice.

Place the shade in the most obvious dark triangular overlap areas and fuzz out. Don't outline overlaps. This causes stripes and stiffness.

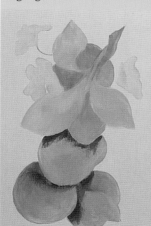

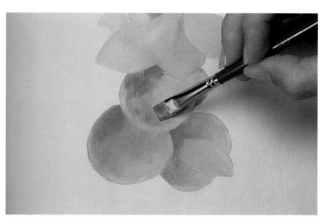

3 Mix the shade color for the plums by mixing the base color with a little more Ivory Black and Prussian Blue. Place this color in the most obvious dark areas—the triangular overlapping areas—and fuzz the color out into the middle area of the plum.

⌘ **HINT** ⌘ *If graphite lines come through the basecoat, place the chisel end of your brush on the graphite line and move the brush back and forth. This will help eliminate those pattern lines.*

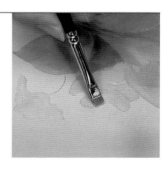

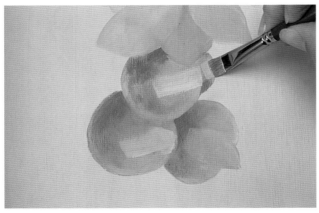

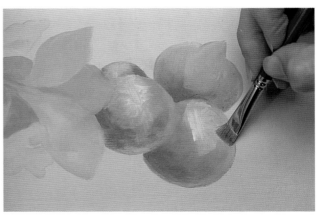

4 Place the highlight on the plum by mixing the base color plus more Titanium White. Pull this color across the fattest part of the plum.

5 Place the brush where the two colors meet and start to blend the highlight out into the middle area.

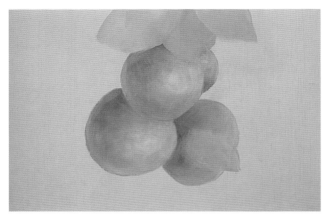

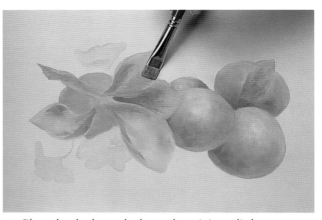

6 Continue to blend the highlight until you have eliminated any hard color breaks. The underneath plum does not get as much detail as the top plums, so it has very little highlight.

7 Place the shade on the leaves by mixing a little more Ivory Black into the base color. Keep this color thin and fuzz it out into the leaf. The more fuzzing you do with the shade color, the easier the blending will be.

⁂HINT⁂ The term "fuzz" refers to the dryness and thinness of the paint. When I fuzz the color out, it's very thin and dry and you can still see the basecoat color coming through.

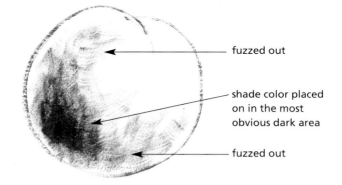

fuzzed out

shade color placed on in the most obvious dark area

fuzzed out

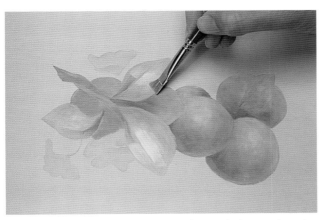

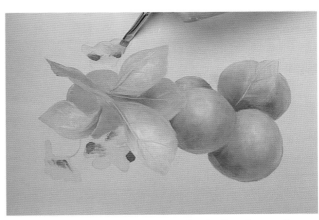

8 Place the highlight in the most obvious light area by mixing more Titanium White and a little Lemon Yellow with the base color. Placing your brush where the two colors meet, start to blend the highlight out and around the surrounding area. If necessary, pick up a little base color to help the transition between the lights and darks.

9 After refining the leaves, place the shade color on the blossoms by mixing Ivory Black and Permanent Alizarin Crimson with the base color. Fuzz this color out.

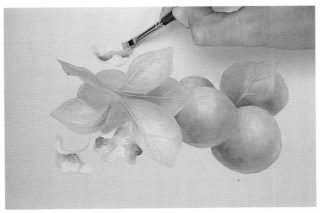

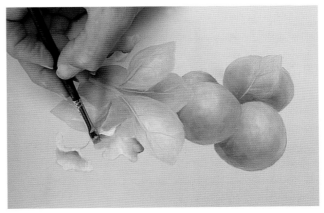

10 Place the highlight on the blossom by mixing more Titanium White into the base color.

11 Blend the highlight. Add some green tints by using a light green leaf mixture. This will help the blossoms relate to the leaves.

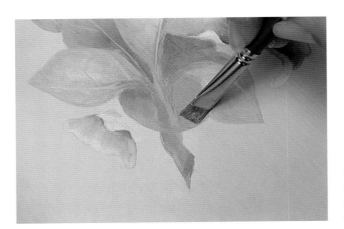

12 When painting an element that has a stem or leaf over it, ignore the stem as you repaint the outside edge of the plum. This will make sure that the outside line of the plum is continuous.

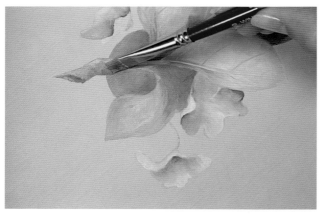

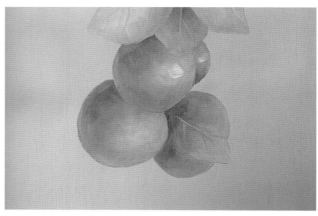

13 Now you can come back and reestablish the stem with dark and light green mixtures. Deepen any shades that need refining.

14 A final sparkle of Titanium White will make this top plum pop out.

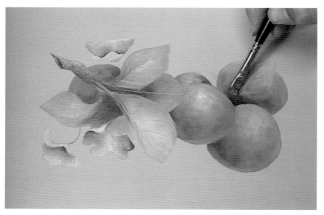

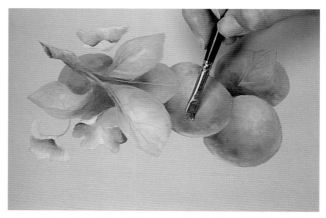

15 Blend the final highlight out, keeping it clean and pure. Add accents of Permanent Alizarin Crimson into the plums. This helps pull the blossoms and the plums together.

16 Place the reflected light on the shadowed side of the plum by using your light leaf mixtures plus more Ivory Black and Titanium White. This will create a cool, light green. Fuzz this color out.

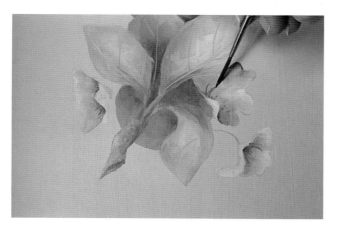

17 Thin the blossom shade color with odorless turpenoid to the consistency of ink. (If you are using water mixable oils, thinning the paint with water may underbind the paint, which keeps it from adhering properly.) Using your liner brush, add detail to the centers of the blossoms. Make the stamens irregular in length, following the contour of the flower. Add the pollen splotches with the green mixtures. Don't get carried away with the stamens and pollen; they should just be suggestions.

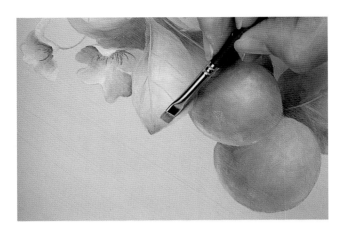

18 Adding tints to the leaves is a perfect way to help pull the elements together. I added the shade color for the blossoms to the tip of this leaf.

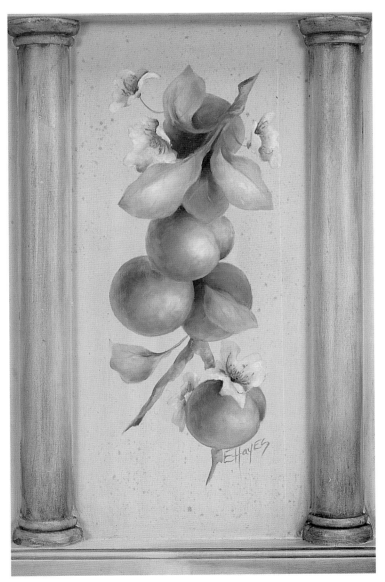

19 Antique the columns of the mirror by brushing on some dark plum mixtures. Rub the columns with a soft cloth, removing the paint on the high areas and keeping the crevices dark. Spatter with light plum mixtures thinned with turpenoid as shown on page 91.

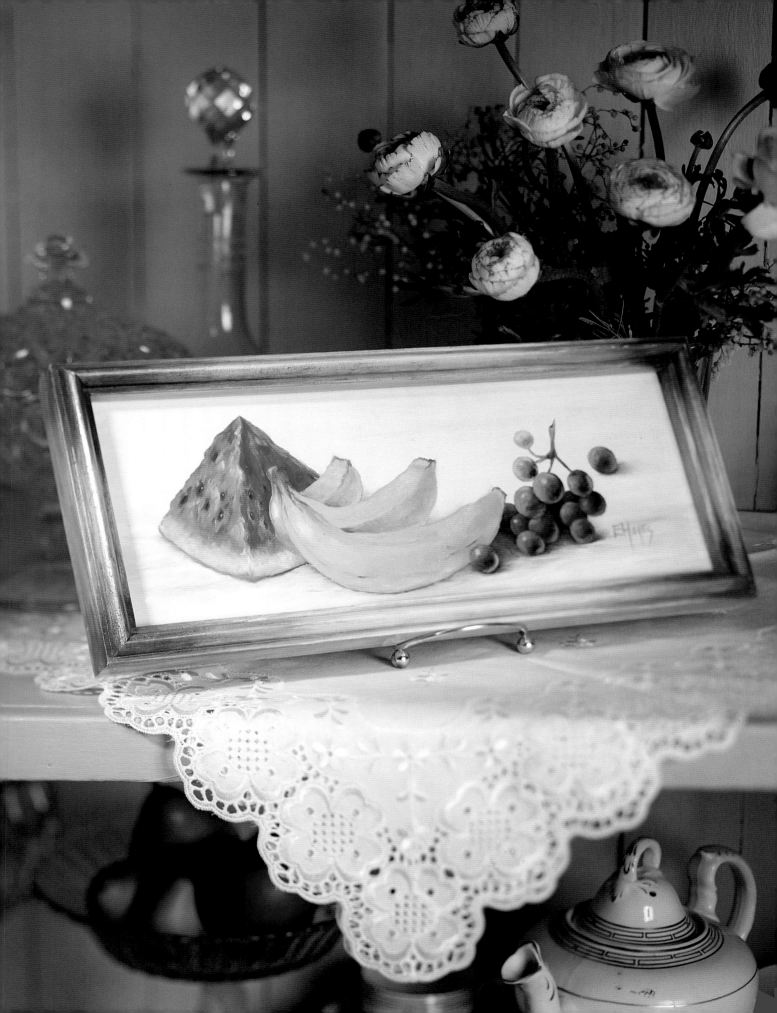

Watermelon, Bananas and Grapes

GRADUATED BLENDING

Graduated blending means blending two values or colors together so there is an even gradation from one to another.

I'm reminded of the college art class I took where I had to take two completely different objects and draw them "morphing" into the other. It was a gradual, step-by-step process as each object became the other. This gave me an admiration for the time and dedication that is involved to refine blending so completely that a painting appears to be photographed. However, I prefer a "choppy refinement" that has vitality and personality.

By not over refining, you can keep freshness in your work. If you over blend your mixes, your paintings will appear stiff and regimented.

Preparing the Background

Basecoat the panel with Delta Ceramcoat White mixed with Jo Sonja's All Purpose Sealer, following the instructions on pages 10-11. Transfer the design.

⇥HINT⇤ *Early on in my painting career, I had three small children and little time or money. One year, instead of painting on wood surfaces that cost me money, I sat down and prepared poster board with acrylic paint and just "fooled around" with my oil paints. I wasn't concerned about messing up, I wasn't intimidated by the cost or size of the piece; in my mind I was just keeping my feet wet while the kids were growing up. One day I would paint strawberries, another day I would paint daisies, and so on. Little did I know that all that experimenting and "fooling around" was the most learning experience of my painting career.*

My advice to you is to sit down with a fifty cent piece of poster board and have some fun. You'll be rewarded with a confidence that will show through in your paintings.

When I sit down to learn a new piece at the piano, I'm never able to play it perfectly the first time through. It takes several hours of practicing before I'm comfortable playing it and can do so without any mistakes. Painting is no different. Don't expect to paint a masterpiece your first time—consider each painting a stepping stone to greater accomplishments.

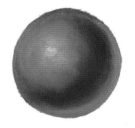

This grape has good darks and lights and an even gradation of color; however, blending too smoothly kills the personality of the grape and makes it look stiff.

A choppier transition between values and colors gives the grape life and personality, making it more interesting. It also gives the suggestion of the "frost" that is often seen on grapes.

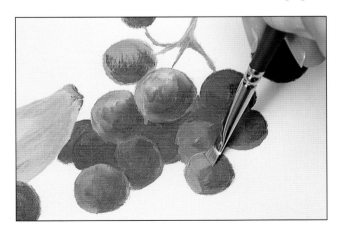

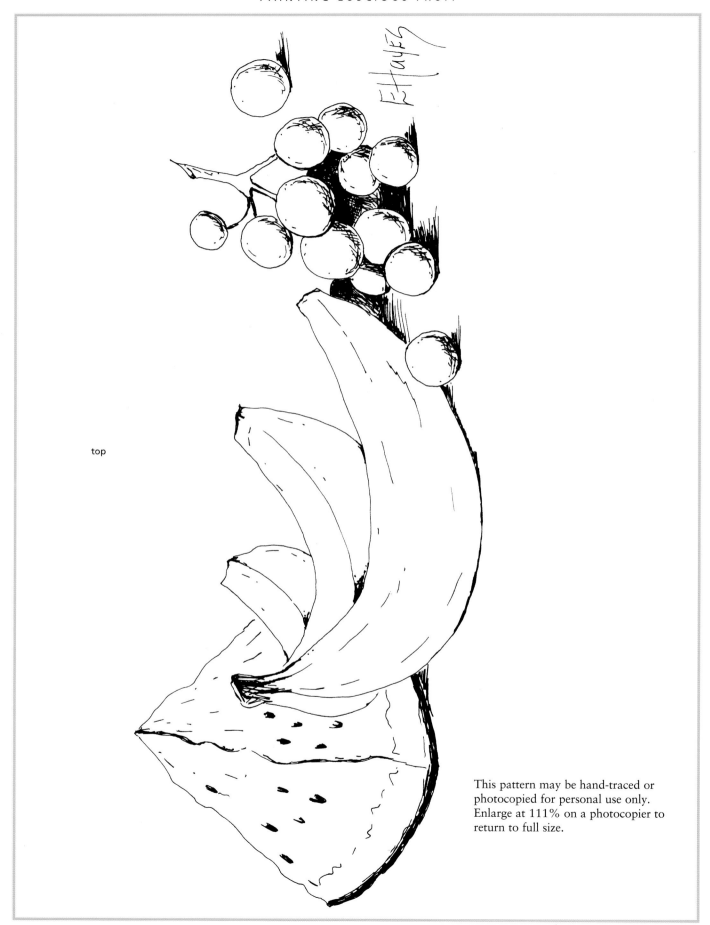

top

This pattern may be hand-traced or photocopied for personal use only. Enlarge at 111% on a photocopier to return to full size.

Materials List

COLOR MIXES

WATERMELON

| **Base**
Cadmium Red Light + Permanent Alizarin Crimson | **White Area**
Titanium White + Yellow Ochre + Lemon Yellow | **Rind**
Cadmium Green Pale | **Shade**
Permanent Alizarin Crimson + Ivory Black | **Highlight**
Titanium White |

BANANAS

| **Base**
Lemon Yellow + Yellow Ochre | **First Shade**
Raw Sienna | **Second Shade**
Raw Sienna + Ivory Black | **Highlight**
Lemon Yellow + Titanium White | **Tint**
Cadmium Green Pale |

BLUE GRAPES

| **Base**
Prussian Blue + Ivory Black + Titanium White | **Shade**
Prussian Blue + Ivory Black | **Highlight**
Base + Titanium White | **Reflected Light**
Prussian Blue + Titanium White | **Sparkle Highlight**
Titanium White |

PURPLE GRAPES

| **Base**
Permanent Alizarin Crimson + Ivory Black + Titanium White | **Shade**
Permanent Alizarin Crimson + Ivory Black | **Highlight**
Base + Titanium White | **Reflected Light**
Cadmium Red Light + Titanium White |

GREEN GRAPES

| **Base**
Cadmium Green Pale | **Shade**
Base + Ivory Black | **Highlight**
Base + Titanium White | **Base**
Cadmium Green Pale | **Antiquing**
Permanent Alizarin Crimson + Ivory Black + Cadmium Green Pale |

FRAME

SURFACE

This shelf is available from Gretchen Cagle Publications, P.O. Box 2104, Claremore, OK 74018-2104. Phone (918) 342-1090 or fax (918) 341-8909.

WINSOR & NEWTON ARTISAN WATER MIXABLE OILS

- Lemon Yellow
- Yellow Ochre
- Raw Sienna
- Cadmium Red Light
- Permanent Alizarin Crimson
- Prussian Blue
- Ivory Black
- Titanium White

TRADITIONAL OILS

- Cadmium Green Pale

BRUSHES

- no. 4, no. 6, no. 8 and no. 10 sable chisel blenders
- no. 1 round sable liner

ADDITIONAL SUPPLIES

- odorless turpenoid
- oil palette
- dark graphite paper
- tracing paper
- ballpoint pen
- Krylon Satin Varnish no. 1701
- Delta Ceramcoat White acrylic
- Winsor & Newton Blending and Glazing Medium
- soft cloth
- 1-inch (2.5cm) sponge brush
- Jo Sonja's All Purpose Sealer
- paper towels
- 220-grit wet/dry sandpaper
- Krylon Matte Finish spray no. 1311

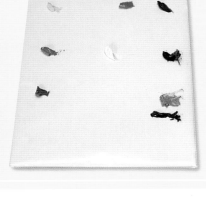

Leave the palette board white since you'll be painting on a white background.

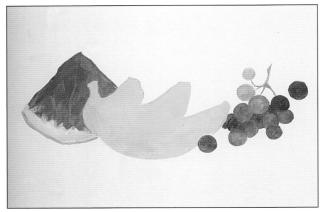

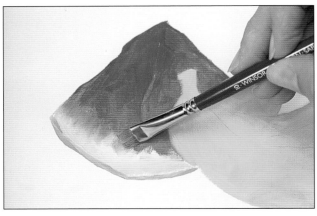

1 Even though the bananas are the foremost element, I chose to start with the watermelon. With a horizontal design such as this, your eye wants to start at the left and continue over to the right as if you were reading. Base the watermelon with Cadmium Red Light plus Permanent Alizarin Crimson. Carefully place in the white part of the meat with Titanium White plus Yellow Ochre and a little Lemon Yellow. Place the rind on with Cadmium Green Pale. Avoid blending these colors together when basing in. Base the bananas with Lemon Yellow plus Yellow Ochre. Base the blue grapes with Prussian Blue plus Ivory Black plus a little Titanium White. Base the purple grapes with Permanent Alizarin Crimson plus Ivory Black plus a little Titanium White. Base the green grapes with Cadmium Green Pale.

2 Using short, choppy, criss-cross strokes carefully blend the white area into the red area.

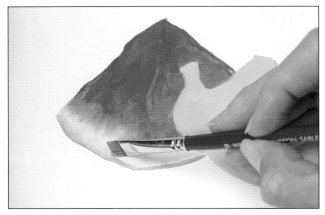

What's Wrong With This Picture?
Even though the three colors in the watermelon rind have an even transition between them, this example shows how overblending can kill the freshness and vitality of the paints. Keeping the transitions between colors a little more choppy will breathe life into your paintings.

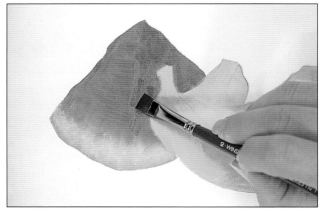

3 Soften the transition between the green rind and the white meat using short, choppy strokes.

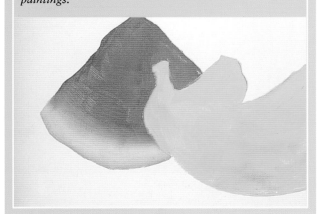

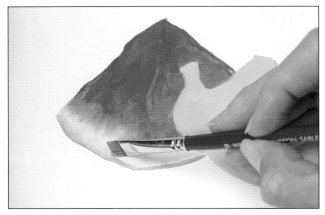

4 Shade the right side of the watermelon with Permanent Alizarin Crimson plus a little Ivory Black. Adding too much black will make the shade color too purple.

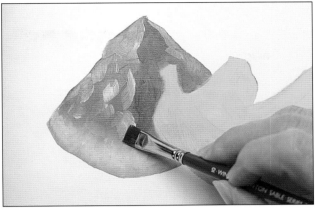

5 Working into a wet basecoat, place the highlight on the left side in irregular splotches with Titanium White.

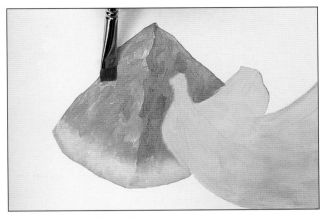

6 Blend the highlight, keeping it choppy.

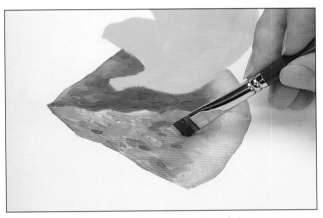

7 Using the corner of your brush and applying pressure, place the seed pockets in with Permanent Alizarin Crimson plus a little Ivory Black. Don't get carried away with these; just a few will do it.

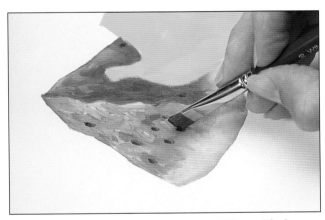

8 Add the seeds in the same manner with Ivory Black.

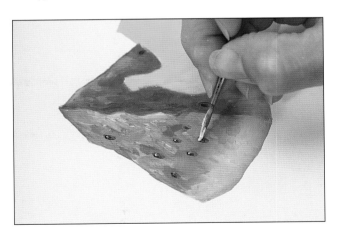

9 With a liner brush and Titanium White, place the shines on the seeds. At this point I spray dried the project so I could refine the banana and grapes with a dried basecoat.

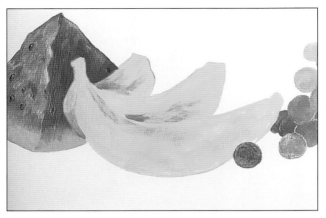

10 Place the shade on the banana in the most obvious dark areas with Raw Sienna and fuzz this color out.

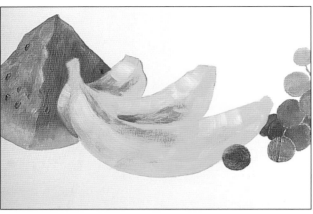

11 Place the highlight on with Lemon Yellow plus Titanium White in the most obvious light areas.

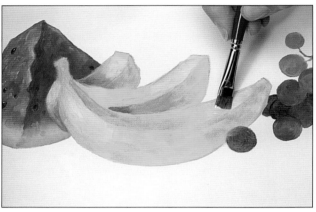

12 Blend the highlight out. I find it necessary at this stage to reapply a little base color to help with the blending between lights and darks.

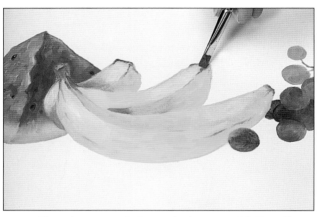

13 Place the accent darks on the banana with Raw Sienna plus Ivory Black, using the chisel end of the brush.

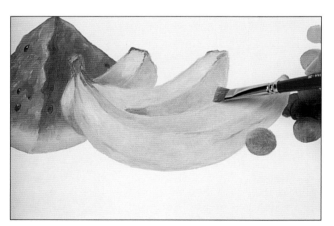

14 Add some green tints on the banana with Cadmium Green Pale

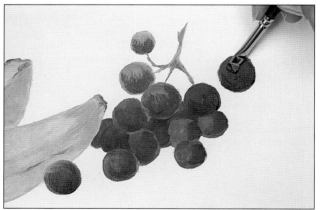

15 Place a crescent-shaped shade on the grapes using Prussian Blue plus Ivory Black for the blue grapes and Permanent Alizarin Crimson plus Ivory Black for the purple grapes. Fuzz out into the middle area. The light source is coming from the upper left, so all shadows will fall on the lower right side with the fattest part of the shadow being in direct line with the light.

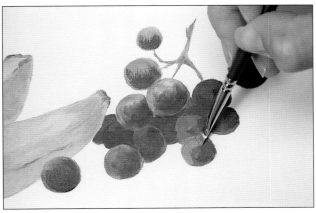

16 Using the original base color plus Titanium White, place the highlight in the most obvious light area. Blend this color out into the middle area with short, choppy strokes.

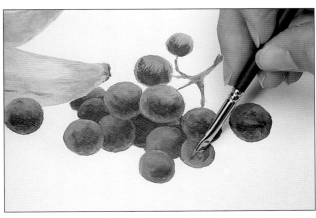

17 Place the reflected light on the shadowed side with Prussian Blue plus Titanium White on the blue grapes and Cadmium Red Light plus Titanium White on the purple grapes. Pull this color out into the shade area, keeping it splotchy.

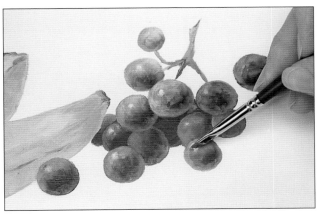

18 Shade and highlight the green grapes and stem in the same manner using Cadmium Green Pale plus Ivory Black for the shade and Cadmium Green Pale plus Titanium White for the light area. Add the sparkle light to the grapes with pure Titanium White and soften the outside edges of the highlight, keeping the center clean and pure.

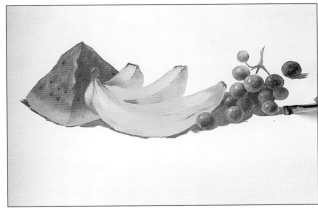

19 Place the cast shadows on the resting surface with Ivory Black, Titanium White and Permanent Alizarin Crimson mixed to a dark, grayed violet.

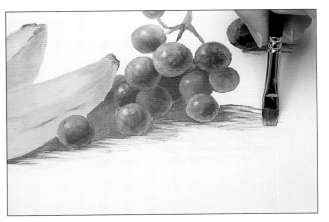

20 Using the chisel end of your brush, chisel back and forth between the cast shadow and the resting surface.

51

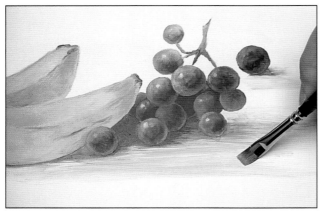

21 Add some Titanium White to the resting surface and continue to chisel back and forth between the cast shadow and the white.

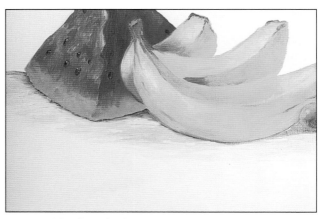

22 Add reflected color into the white resting surface by using the watermelon base color for the watermelon area, the banana base color around the bananas and the grape base colors near the grapes.

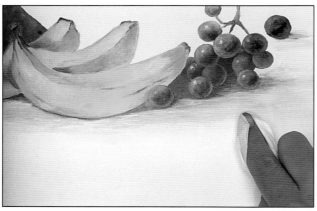

23 Soften the outer edges of these reflected accents with a soft cloth so that they gradually disappear.

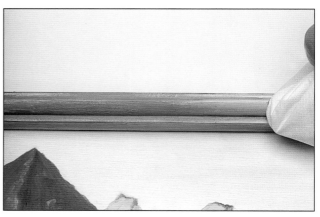

24 Brush Cadmium Green Pale on the frame. Use a soft cloth to remove most of the color, keeping color in the grooves.

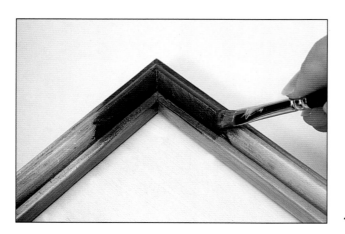

25 Paint the corners of the frame with Permanent Alizarin Crimson plus Cadmium Green Pale.

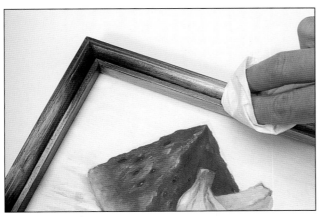

26 Soften the transition between this darker shade and the original Cadmium Green Pale color by rubbing with a soft cloth. Keep the corners dark, gradually fading away.

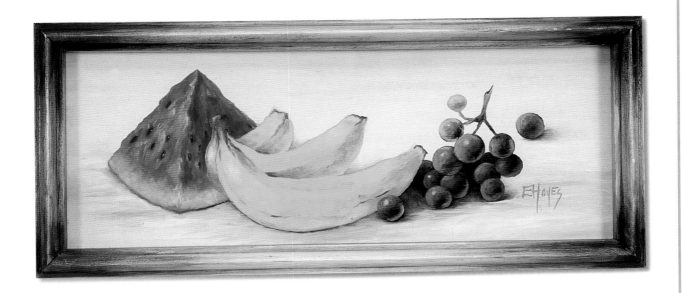

27 What I like most about this painting is its painterly quality, freshness and vitality. The elements are painted in a convincing manner, yet are not overblended to resemble a photograph. There is enough choppiness in the blending to create personality and life.

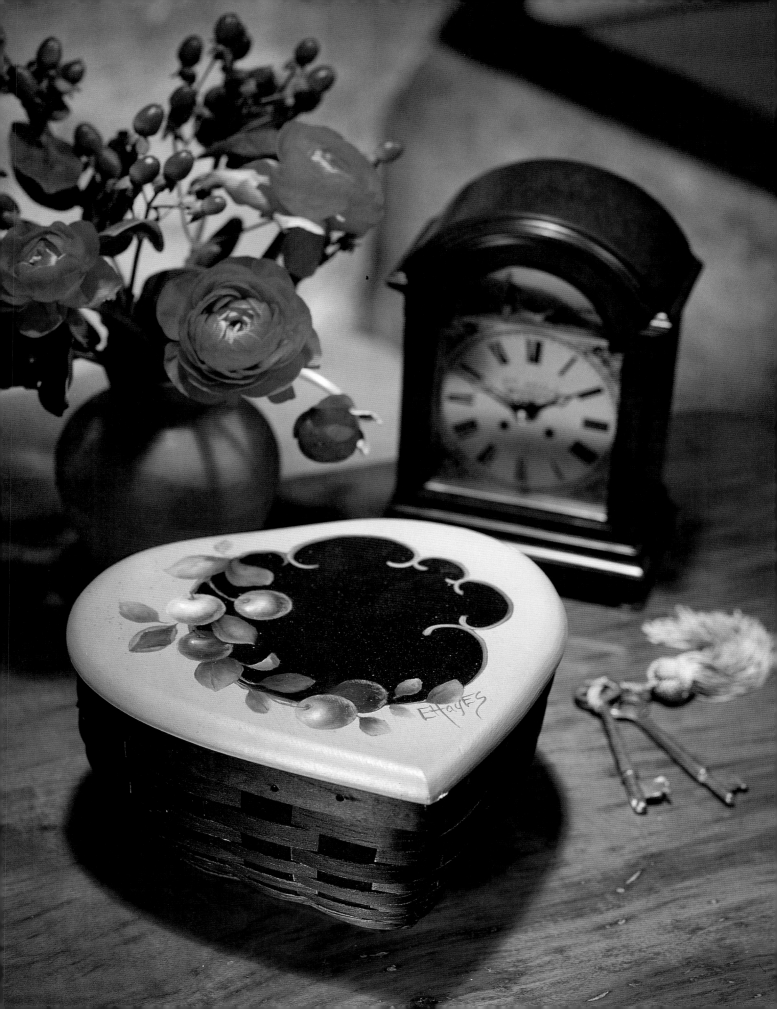

Cherries

BACKGROUND VALUES

Look at the two bands of ochre color at right. Which one appears darker?

As you can see in the third sample, they're actually the same color, but the difference in background values creates the illusion that the band on the light background is darker than the same color band on a dark background. The environment in which your colors exist dictates their characteristics.

Combining background colors is an excellent way to learn how value and color affect the handling of the paint. It also creates more interest within the painting.

Analyzing Your Values

Whenever I mix a color on my palette and lay it down on my painting, I immediately analyze it in relationship to its surroundings before I continue to add more paint. Is it too light, too dark, too warm or too cool? After analyzing the color, and adjusting if necessary, I continue with my painting.

If you're not sure whether you have enough or too much value change in your finished painting, make a black-and-white photocopy of the piece to eliminate color and all you will see are the values.

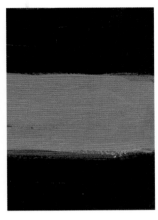

Which ochre band appears darker? At first glance, the color on the light green background appears darker.

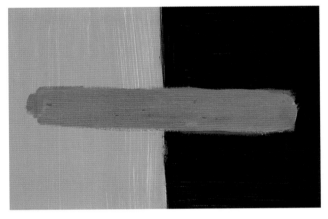

As you can see here, it is actually the same color. The value of the background greatly influences the characteristics of a color.

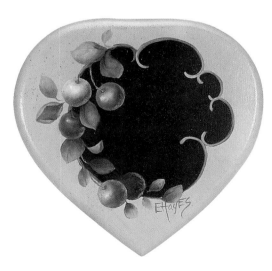

To see if you have enough value change within your painting, make a black-and-white photocopy of it. Now you can analyze the values better without the colors getting in the way. If you don't see a lot of value change between the darks and lights, refine the painting further.

Preparing the Background

Basecoat and seal the lid with Delta Ceramcoat Wedgwood Green acrylic. When dry, transfer the outline of the circle design. Paint the inside of this circle with Delta Ceramcoat Black acrylic. When dry, sand lightly to eliminate any ridges between colors. Transfer the design. Spray the rest of the basket with a black spray paint.

◆HINT ◆ *When opening a new tube of oil paint, spray the cap with non-stick cooking spray. This will stop any paint from drying around the cap and making it hard to screw back on.*

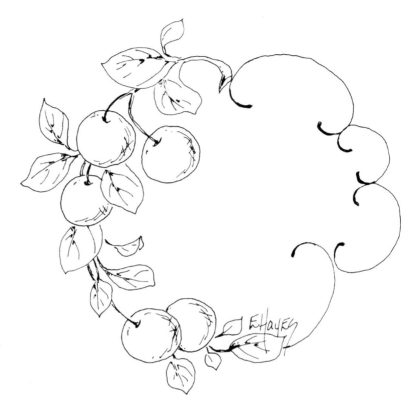

This pattern may be hand-traced or photocopied for personal use only. Enlarge 143% on a photocopier to return to full size.

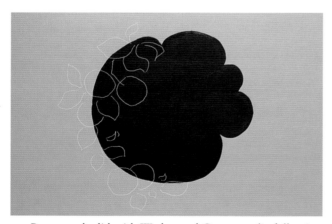

1 Basecoat the lid with Wedgwood Green acrylic following the instructions on pages 10-11. Transfer the outline of the circle design and paint the inset with Black acrylic. Sand between the colors to eliminate any ridges. Transfer the pattern.

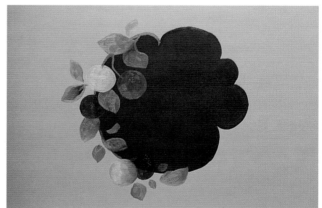

2 Basecoat the yellow cherries with Yellow Ochre plus Lemon Yellow plus Titanium White. Base the medium value cherries with Permanent Alizarin Crimson plus Cadmium Red Light plus a little Titanium White. Base the dark cherries with Permanent Alizarin Crimson plus Ivory Black. Base the leaves in various values and temperatures that are appropriate for the background using Ivory Black plus Lemon Yellow plus Titanium White. Spray dry.

Materials List

COLOR MIXES

LIGHT CHERRY

Base	**Shade**	**Highlight**
Yellow Ochre + Lemon Yellow + Titanium White	Permanent Alizarin Crimson + Raw Sienna	Base + Lemon Yellow

MEDIUM CHERRY

Base	**Shade**	**Highlight**
Permanent Alizarin Crimson + Cadmium Red Light + Titanium White	Permanent Alizarin Crimson + Ivory Black	Base + Titanium White

DARK CHERRY

ALL CHERRIES

Base	**Shade**	**Highlight**	**Reflected Light**
Permanent Alizarin Crimson + Ivory Black	Base + Ivory Black	Permanent Alizarin Crimson + Cadmium Red Light + Titanium White	Ivory Black + Titanium White

LEAVES ON LIGHT BACKGROUND

Base	**Shade**	**Highlight**
Ivory Black + Lemon Yellow + Titanium White	Base + Ivory Black	Base + Titanium White

LEAVES ON DARK BACKGROUND

Base	**Shade**	**Highlight**
same as Light Background Base except add more Ivory Black + a little Permanent Alizarin Crimson	same as Light Background Shade except add more Ivory Black + a little Permanent Alizarin Crimson	same as Light Background except add more Ivory Black + a little Permanent Alizarin Crimson

SURFACE

This basket is available from The Pesky Bear, 5059 Roszyk Hill Road, Machias, NY 14101. Phone (716) 942-3250.

WINSOR & NEWTON ARTISAN WATER MIXABLE OILS

- Lemon Yellow
- Yellow Ochre
- Raw Sienna
- Cadmium Red Light
- Permanent Alizarin Crimson
- Ivory Black
- Titanium White

BRUSHES

- no. 4, no. 6 and no. 8 sable chisel blenders
- no. 1 round sable liner

ADDITIONAL SUPPLIES

- Delta Ceramcoat Wedgwood Green acrylic
- Delta Ceramcoat Black acrylic
- ½-inch (1.3cm) sponge brush
- paper towels
- 220-grit wet/dry sandpaper
- Jo Sonja's All Purpose Sealer
- Krylon Matte Finish spray no. 1311
- odorless turpenoid
- oil palette
- light graphite paper
- tracing paper
- ballpoint pen
- black spray paint
- Krylon Satin Varnish no. 1701

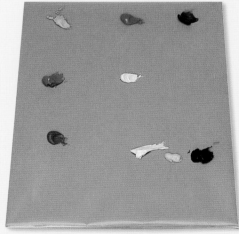

Basecoat the palette board with Wedgwood Green acrylic.

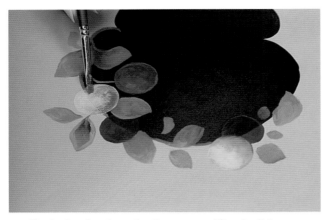

3 Shade the cherries using Permanent Alizarin Crimson plus Raw Sienna for the yellow cherries and Permanent Alizarin Crimson plus Ivory Black for the darker cherries. Keep the color thin and fuzzy as it nears the middle of the cherry.

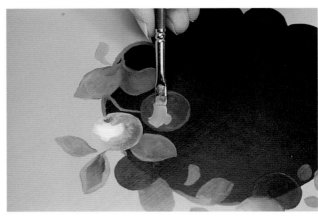

4 Place the highlight across the fat part of the cherries. For the yellow and middle value cherries, use the base color plus Titanium White. For the darkest cherries, highlight with Permanent Alizarin Crimson plus Cadmium Red Light plus a little Titanium White.

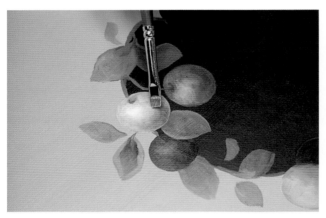

5 Blend the highlight. If necessary, pick up a little base color to help the blending.

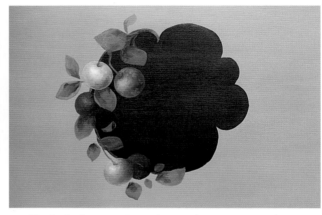

6 Shade the leaves using values and temperatures that are appropriate for each leaf.

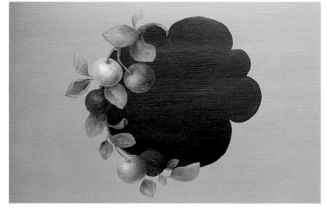

7 Highlight the leaves using values and temperatures that are appropriate for each leaf.

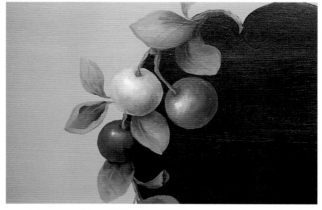

8 Add a sparkle of Titanium White to each cherry. Don't over blend this sparkle.

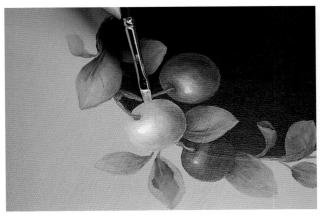

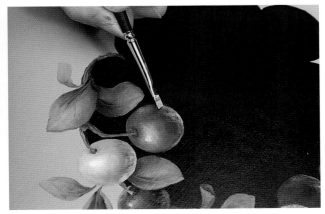

9 Add some subtle green tints on the cherries using greens from the leaves.

10 Add reflected light on the dark side of the cherries using Ivory Black plus Titanium White. Keep this color dry and splotchy.

What's Wrong With This Picture?
The little leaves at the bottom of the design aren't value appropriate for their background.

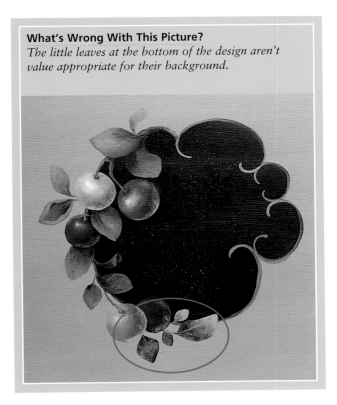

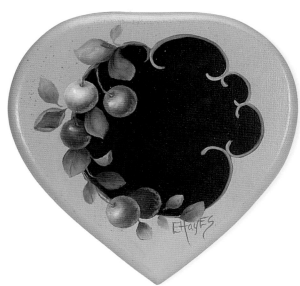

11 Thin down some greens from the leaves with odorless turpenoid and add the scrollwork with a liner brush. Spatter with this same mixture, following the instructions on page 91.

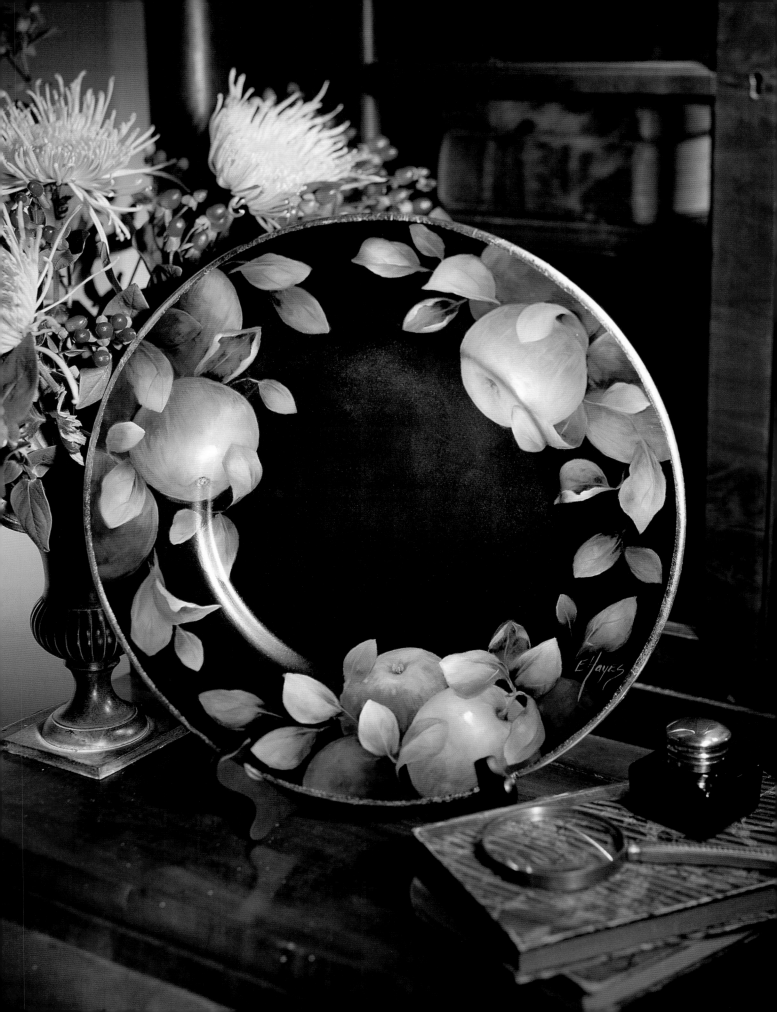

Apples All Around

DEVELOPING DEPTH AND DIMENSION

Value and temperature change between elements create depth and dimension. Without them you have flatness and monotony.

Can you imagine what life would look like if flowers were all the same color, if they had no lights and no darks? Imagine never seeing the sunlight glistening on an apple as it sways on the tree. Life would indeed be very flat and boring.

The challenge is to create three-dimensional objects on a two-dimensional surface. When I begin painting a design, I concentrate on three things. First, choosing the correct hue, or color. If I'm painting apples, I first must choose whether I'm going to paint a red, green or yellow apple.

Once I've decided on colors, I concentrate on value. Let's say I'm painting a red apple. Is my apple going to be a light red or a dark red? I mix my colors accordingly.

The last question is what temperature is my apple? By this I mean is it a warm red or a cool red. Do I want my apple to be a red that leans toward the orange family, which would make it a warmer red or a true red, or one that leans toward the violet family which would make it a cooler red.

Understanding color theory is vital at this stage of the game. Invest in a color wheel and a book on color theory and familiarize yourself with the properties of each color and their relationships to one another.

As I begin painting a design, I always start with my focal point and work down in planes. This way I can relate everything to the focal point and not relate the focal point to everything else.

As I start to base in the top elements I ask myself what color, value and temperature they are. Generally I'll paint the elements that are in the foreground light, bright and warm. As I work down in planes and the elements are getting further away from me, I'll adjust my colors so that they are darker, duller and cooler. By doing this in the beginning stages you automatically start to get a sense of depth.

If I've done my job right in these beginning stages then my detail stage is a snap. As I begin to detail I'm adding dimension to my painting by concentrating on developing light areas that come toward the viewer and shadowed areas that move away from the viewer. Always ask yourself how an element is affected by light.

Preparing the Background

Basecoat the tin plate with Delta Ceramcoat Black acrylic. Transfer the design.

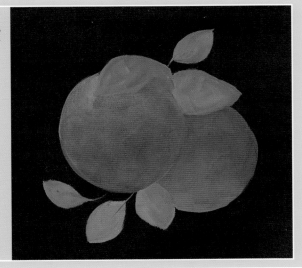

What's Wrong With This Picture?
These apples and leaves were all basecoated with the same value and temperature. This makes them appear very flat, as if they all exist on the same plane. Changing values and temperatures will give the illusion of depth.

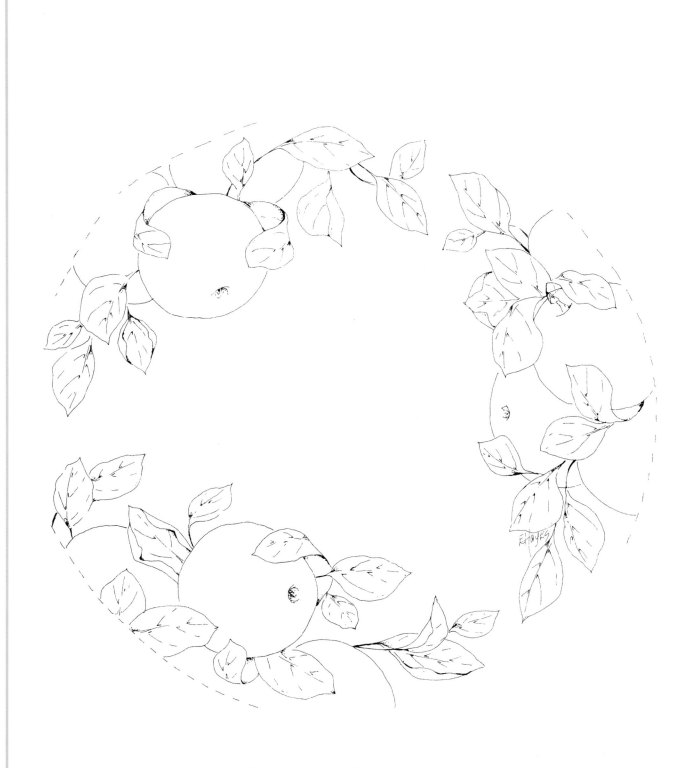

This pattern may be hand-traced or photocopied for personal use only. Enlarge 213% on a photocopier to return to full size.

Materials List

COLOR MIXES

APPLES

Base
Yellow Ochre +
Cadmium Green
Pale

Shade
Permanent
Alizarin Crimson
+ Ivory Black

Shade
Cadmium Green
Pale + Ivory
Black

Light
Base + Cadmium
Green Pale +
Titanium White

Highlight
Light + Lemon
Yellow + more
Titanium White

Reflected Light
Ivory Black +
Titanium White

LEAVES

Base
Ivory Black +
Oxide of
Chromium +
Lemon Yellow

Shade
Base + Ivory
Black + a little
Permanent
Alizarin Crimson

Warm Light
Base + Lemon
Yellow +
Titanium White

Cool Light
Base + Titanium
White

SURFACE

This tin plate is available from Carolyn's Folk Art Studio, P.O. Box 624, Matthews, NC 38106. Phone (704) 847-0487.

WINSOR & NEWTON ARTISAN WATER MIXABLE OILS

- Cadmium Lemon
- Yellow Ochre
- Raw Sienna
- Cadmium Red Light
- Permanent Alizarin Crimson
- Prussian Blue
- Ivory Black
- Titanium White

TRADITIONAL OILS

- Oxide of Chromium
- Cadmium Green Pale

BRUSHES

- no. 6, no. 8 and no. 10 sable chisel blenders
- no. 1 round sable liner

ADDITIONAL SUPPLIES

- Delta Ceramcoat Black acrylic
- Jo Sonja's All Purpose Sealer
- ½-inch (1.3cm) sponge brush
- paper towels
- 220-grit wet/dry sandpaper
- gold leaf adhesive
- odorless turpenoid

- oil palette
- light-colored graphite paper
- tracing paper
- ballpoint pen
- Krylon Satin Varnish no. 1701
- gold leaf sheets
- bristle brush
- Krylon Matte Finish spray no. 1311

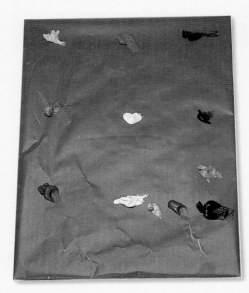

Basecoat the palette board with Black acrylic.

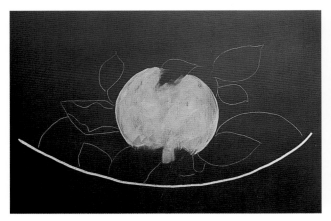

1 Basecoat the top apple with Yellow Ochre plus Cadmium Green Pale.

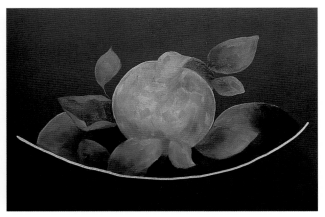

2 Basecoat the leaves using various values and temperatures of Ivory Black plus Oxide of Chromium plus a little Lemon Yellow. Block in the darker apples using Permanent Alizarin Crimson plus Ivory Black in the dark areas and Yellow Ochre plus Cadmium Green Pale in the light areas. Notice that some of my dark areas are as dark as the background. Spray dry.

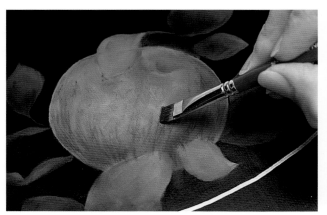

3 Using Permanent Alizarin Crimson and a little Ivory Black, place a crescent-shaped shade on the top apple. Keep this color thin and fuzzy. Using the chisel end of your brush, begin pulling this shade color up into the apple following the apple's contour. Using Cadmium Green Pale and a little Ivory Black, shade the blossom end of the apple.

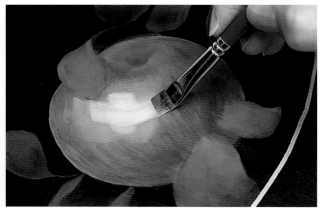

4 Begin highlighting by mixing more Cadmium Green Pale and Titanium White into the base color. When highlighting, it's important to gradually step up in values. Here I've placed on a value slightly lighter than the basecoat. I then applied another layer of highlight within that area that is slightly lighter than the previous color. I created this color by adding a little Lemon Yellow and Titanium White to the first highlight color.

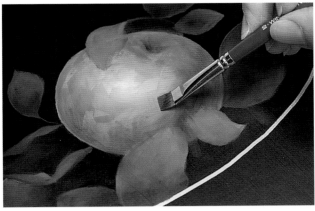

5 Blend the highlight color out into the apple. Pick up a little base color if necessary to help with the blending.

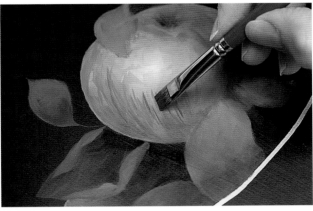

6 Add streaks to the apple by using the chisel end of your brush and a little Permanent Alizarin Crimson. Make sure you follow the contour of the apple.

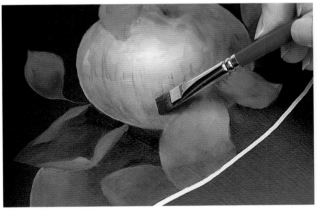

7 Soften the streaks by lightly blending across them.

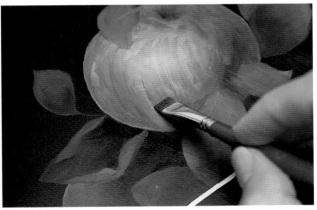

8 With a dry brush, pull down the apple following the contour. Dry wipe your brush between each stroke.

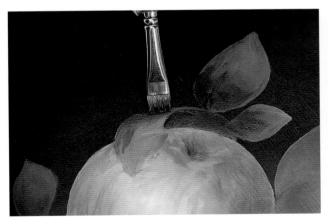

9 Shade the leaves using a value that is darker than the base color.

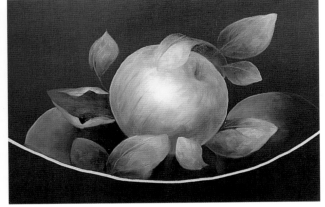

10 Highlight the leaves by adding more Lemon Yellow and Titanium White to the base color. Keep the top leaves warmer and brighter and the bottom leaves duller and darker.

What's Wrong With This Picture?

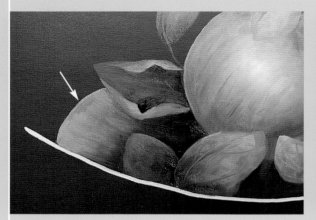

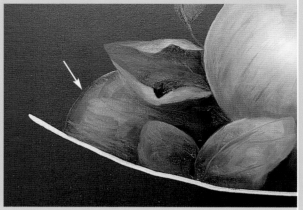

The outside edge of the underneath apple is too light, making the apple look flat.

Darkening the outside edge gives the illusion that the apple edge is rolling away from you.

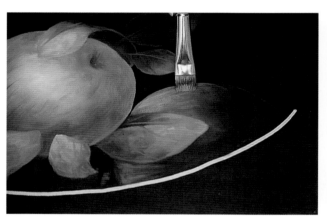

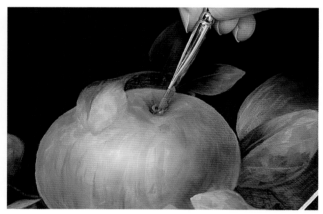

11 Lighten the underneath apples by adding a little Yellow Ochre plus Cadmium Green Pale plus a little Titanium White. Don't get too light with this color.

12 Place the detail in the blossom end by using the chisel end of the brush and a little Yellow Ochre.

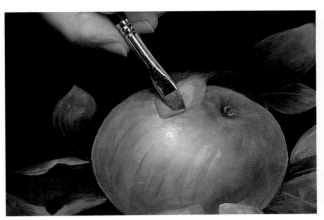 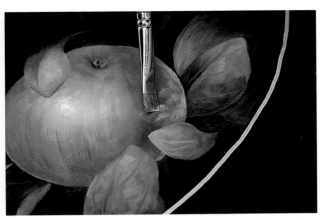

13 Place a strong sparkle highlight on the apple with Titanium White. To create more contrast between the apple and the leaf, darken the tip of the leaf with a darker green mix. This will help pull the eye toward this area, making it the focal point.

14 Place the reflected light on the dark side of the apple with Ivory Black plus Titanium White. Keep this color dry and choppy.

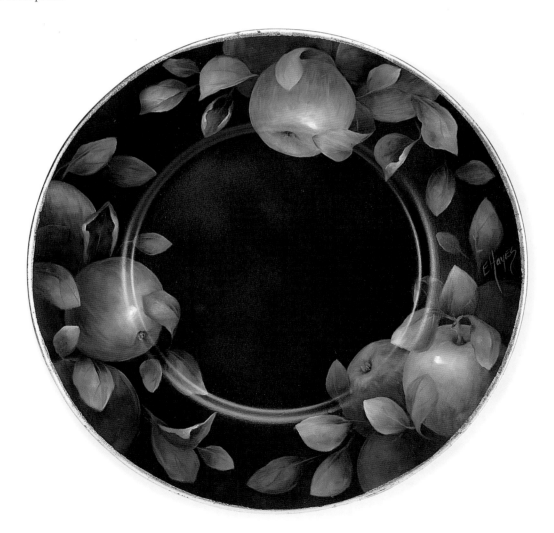

15 Gold leaf a small band around the outside edge of the plate, following the instructions on page 90. Varnish and enjoy.

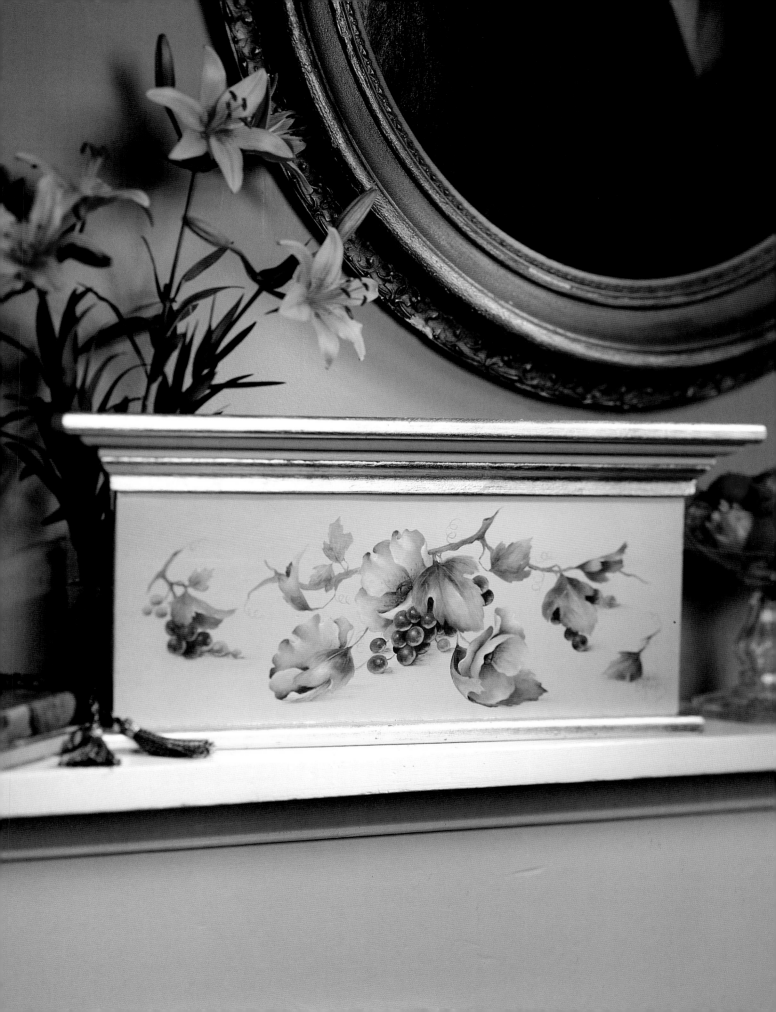

Grapes and Poppies

TINTS AND ACCENTS

Tints are colors that have been mixed with white. Accents are done with pure pigments. The purpose of tints and accents are to help pull the elements together so that they relate to one another and to help carry your eye throughout the design.

Many students find themselves in a dilemma about where to put a tint or accent in the design. However, the only *wrong* place to put a tint or accent is in a highlight area. Everywhere else is fair game.

Leaves are a perfect area in which to place some tints and accents because you can incorporate the fruit or flower color either in the shade area or on an outside edge to help relate the two elements together. If you add tints or accents to your leaves, also place some leaf color somewhere in the fruits or flowers, thus tying the painting together.

Preparing the Background

Basecoat the surface using a mixture of Delta Ceramcoat Sandstone and Jo Sonja's All Purpose Sealer, following the instructions on pages 10-11. Transfer the design.

Materials List

SURFACE
This shelf is available from Gretchen Cagle Publications, P.O. Box 2104, Claremore, OK 74018-2104. Phone (918) 342-1090 or fax (918) 341-8909.

WINSOR & NEWTON ARTISAN WATER MIXABLE OILS
- Lemon Yellow
- Yellow Ochre
- Raw Sienna
- Cadmium Red Light
- Permanent Alizarin Crimson
- Prussian Blue
- Ivory Black
- Titanium White

BRUSHES
- no. 6, no. 8 and no. 10 sable chisel blenders
- no. 1 round sable liner

ADDITIONAL SUPPLIES
- Delta Ceramcoat Sandstone acrylic
- Delta Ceramcoat Red Iron Oxide acrylic
- 1-inch (2.5cm) sponge brush
- 220-grit wet/dry sandpaper
- Jo Sonja's All Purpose Sealer
- Krylon Matte Finish spray no. 1311
- odorless turpenoid
- paper towels
- disposable palette for oils
- dark graphite paper
- tracing paper
- ballpoint pen
- gold leaf adhesive
- gold leaf sheets
- bristle brush
- Krylon Satin Varnish no. 1701

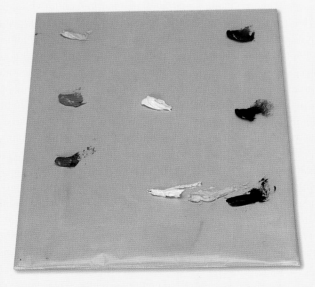

Basecoat the palette board with Sandstone acrylic.

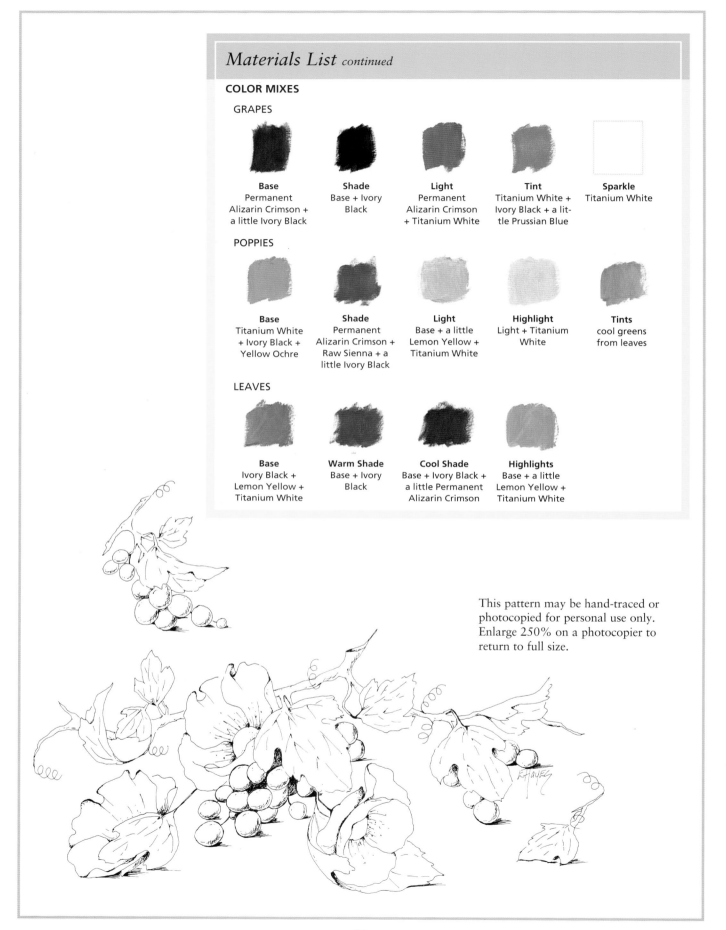

Materials List *continued*

COLOR MIXES

GRAPES

Base
Permanent Alizarin Crimson + a little Ivory Black

Shade
Base + Ivory Black

Light
Permanent Alizarin Crimson + Titanium White

Tint
Titanium White + Ivory Black + a little Prussian Blue

Sparkle
Titanium White

POPPIES

Base
Titanium White + Ivory Black + Yellow Ochre

Shade
Permanent Alizarin Crimson + Raw Sienna + a little Ivory Black

Light
Base + a little Lemon Yellow + Titanium White

Highlight
Light + Titanium White

Tints
cool greens from leaves

LEAVES

Base
Ivory Black + Lemon Yellow + Titanium White

Warm Shade
Base + Ivory Black

Cool Shade
Base + Ivory Black + a little Permanent Alizarin Crimson

Highlights
Base + a little Lemon Yellow + Titanium White

This pattern may be hand-traced or photocopied for personal use only. Enlarge 250% on a photocopier to return to full size.

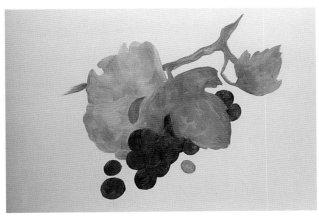

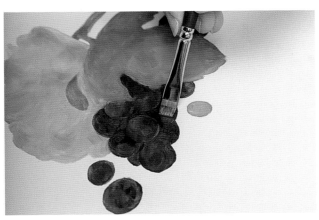

1 Base in the grapes with Permanent Alizarin Crimson plus a little Ivory Black. Base in the leaves and stems with Ivory Black plus Lemon Yellow plus Titanium White. Use various values and temperatures throughout the leaves. Base in the poppies with Titanium White plus a little Yellow Ochre plus a little Ivory Black. After basing everything in, soften all the hard edges and erase any smudges with the kneaded eraser. Spray dry.

2 Place a crescent-shaped shade on the dark side of the grapes with the base color plus a little more Ivory Black. Fuzz this color out into the middle of the grape.

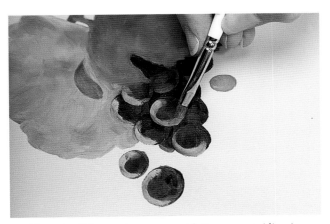

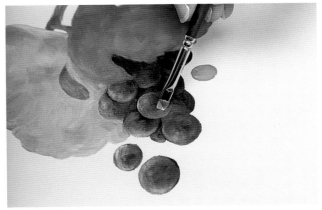

3 Place the light on the grapes with Permanent Alizarin Crimson plus Titanium White.

4 Blend this light tone into the grapes. If you overblend and lose the light, replace it and start again. The advantage to working on a dry basecoat is that this light mix should not blend away.

⋈HINT ⋈ *When is white not just white? When using paint to record white objects. The biggest mistake I see in my teaching is that most students can't visualize dark tones of white. It's easy to visualize dark and light tones of blue, but when it comes to white, we think of just one tone. The trick to painting white objects is to start dull and dirty. Use lots of color variations. By having a dull and dirty basecoat, your white highlights will stand out better.*

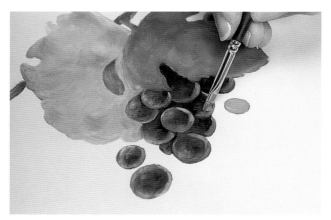

5 Place the reflected light on with Titanium White plus Ivory Black plus a little Prussian Blue. Spray dry.

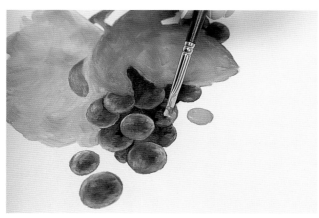

6 Pull the reflected light into the grapes with short, choppy strokes, keeping the color splotchy.

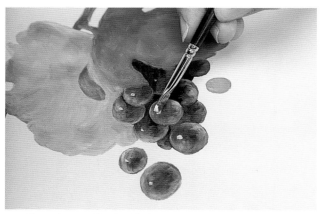

7 Place the sparkle highlight with pure Titanium White. Notice the placement of this sparkle and how it appears only on the grapes that are in the foreground and are directly in line with the light source.

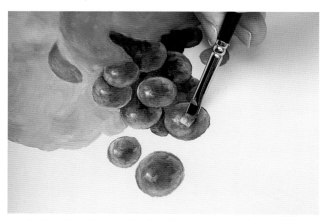

8 Soften the edges of this highlight, keeping the sparkle clean and pure in the center.

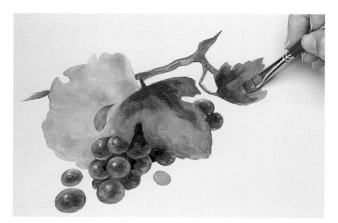

9 Shade the leaf with the original base color plus a little more Ivory Black plus a little Permanent Alizarin Crimson. (This begins to add some accent colors to the leaves that relate to the grapes.) Keep this color thin and fuzzy.

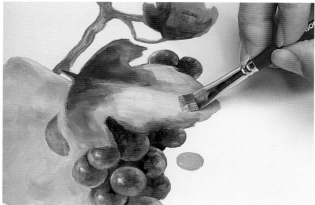

10 Begin placing the highlight on the leaf with the base color plus a little more Lemon Yellow plus Titanium White. Be careful not to jump too fast in value with the highlight; it should be a gradual process of adding lights.

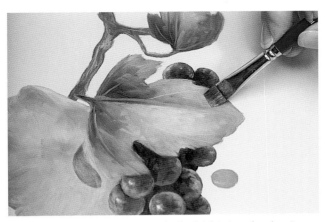

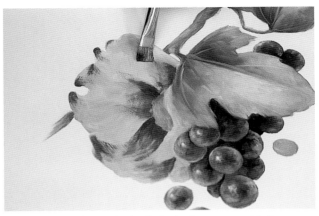

11 Blend the highlight on the leaf. This is a focal point leaf so it receives a lot of attention. As you continue throughout the design, leaves that are further away from the focal point are less important and should receive less detail.

12 After refining the leaf, shade the poppy with Permanent Alizarin Crimson plus Raw Sienna plus a little Ivory Black. Once again, place the color in the most obvious dark areas and then fuzz out.

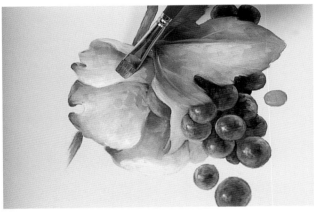

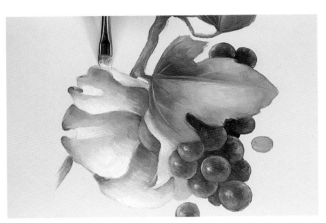

13 Begin lightening the poppy with the original base color plus a little Lemon Yellow and Titanium White. Be careful not to jump too fast with the whites; adding too much white too fast will make the flower look milky and dead. A white flower needs to have some dirty colors in it so that the highlights can hold their own.

14 Continue gradually adding more highlights.

What's Wrong With This Picture?

Can you see the dark stripe between the petals in the left picture? This happens when applying a dark color all along an overlap. The easiest way to fix stripes between elements is to blend across the stripe, getting rid of any hard color breaks. Next, come back and reestablish the top petal by adding a lighter tone. There is still dark near the center and dark near the triangular area where the petal edges overlap, but the middle area is closer in value and is softer on the eyes.

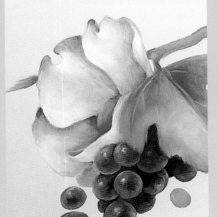

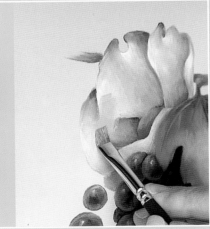

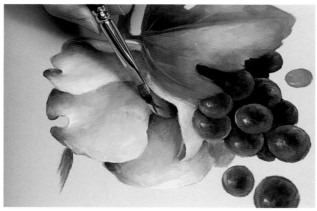

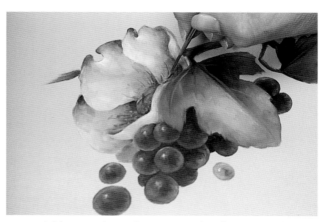

15 Add some shade to the poppy center where it disappears into the forward petal using your green mixtures. Next, create the detail in the poppy center by painting an X with the chisel end of your brush.

16 Add suggestions of stamens and pollen using a liner brush with green mixtures that are value appropriate. Getting them too dark or too light will make them jump out at you.

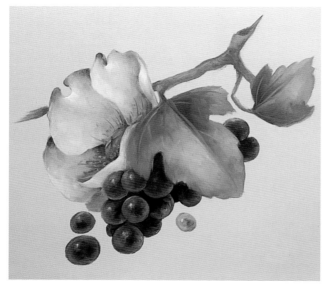

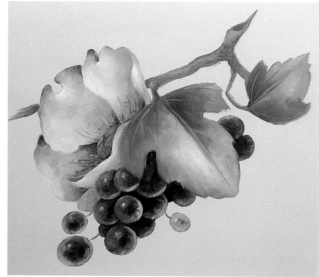

17 Once I refine to a certain point, I step back and analyze what I've done. Looking at this painting I see my poppy highlights have become the focal point—they are the first thing my eye is drawn to. I could either tone down the highlights on the poppy or boost up the highlights on the leaves and grapes. I chose to boost the highlights on the leaves and reinforce the reflected light on the grapes. Now the first thing you see are the grapes because the value change between the reflected light and the darks of the other grapes is the greatest. Strong value change between elements will always draw your eye to that area. Next, I need to add some tints to the elements so that they relate better to one another. The poppy already has some grape color in the shade areas, so add some greens from the leaves to the poppy. Next, add some greens to the grapes. The leaves already have some grape accent color in the shade. If this is not noticeable, add a little more Permanent Alizarin Crimson to the shade color. Tints and accents can be added to any dark or middle value area. Never place a tint or accent in a highlight area.

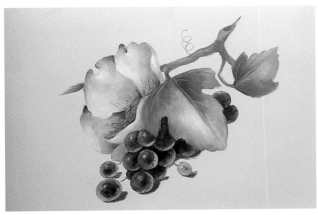

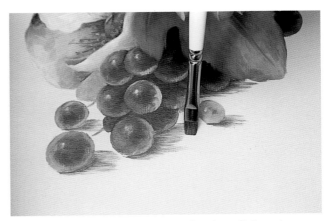

18 Add the tendrils with thinned down green mixtures and a liner brush. Place the resting shadows on with Ivory Black, Titanium White and a little Permanent Alizarin Crimson. This is a dark, grayed violet.

19 Using the chisel end of your brush, pull the color out, keeping it horizontal.

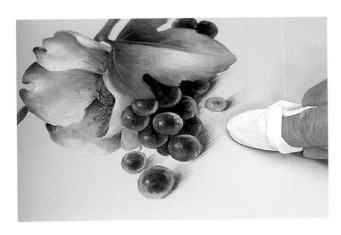

20 Soften the outer edges of the shadows with a soft cloth. There should be varying degrees of value within this resting shadow, with the darkest area lying next to the grapes.

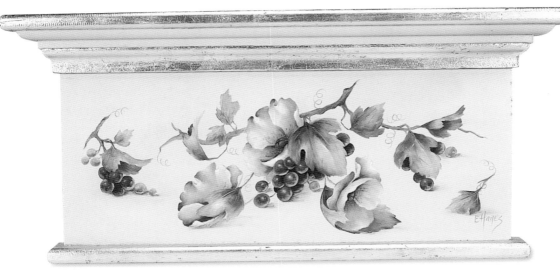

21 See how the tints and accents throughout this design help carry your eye from one element to another? Everything is related. Be careful not to get carried away with these tints and accents or they will start looking spotty and your eye won't know where to look first. To finish this project, gold leaf the trim and outside edges of the shelf following the instructions shown on page 90. Varnish and enjoy.

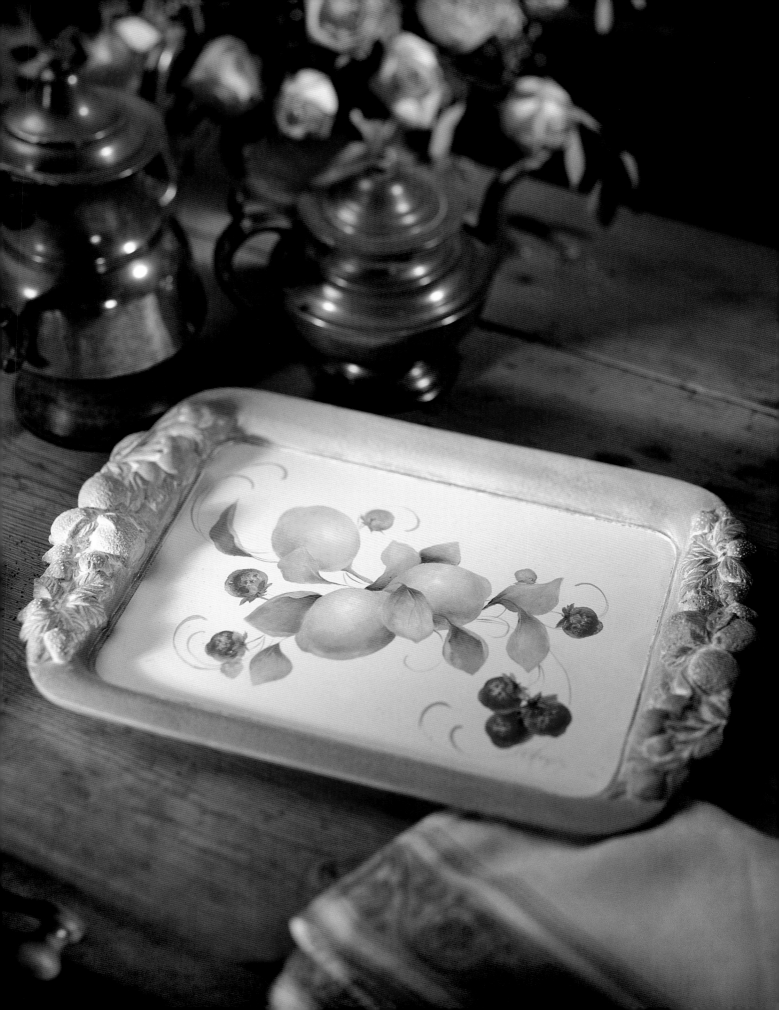

Lemons and Strawberries

SETTING THE MOOD WITH THE BACKGROUND

Background colors set the mood for your painting. As you look at the finished project at left and the three samples on page 78, you should get a different feeling from each one. However, all four paintings contain the same three basic colors: yellows for the lemons, reds for the strawberries and greens for the leaves. The difference lies within the background choice.

Using different background colors forces you to handle the yellows and greens differently. This is important because the painting needs to coexist with its surroundings and not just lay on top of it. It needs to be a part of it and not look as if it was cut-out and pasted on.

It would be impossible for me to give you one color setup for lemons and expect you to paint lemons every time with that same color setup. The elements surrounding the lemons, as well as the background choice, influences their color.

Let's analyze the four paintings and determine how each was painted to coexist with its background.

Bright and Cheery

Although the lemons in the painting at left are relatively warm, they are not quite as warm as the lemons in the warm and colorful painting on page 78. The cooler background color warrants using cooler colors in both the lemons and leaves.

The value of the shade color on the lemons is quite a bit lighter than the shade in the dark and dramatic painting. Your darkest dark needs to be as dark as your background, so if I'm painting on a light background, I can keep my colors relatively light. If I'm painting on a dark background, some area of the painting needs to be very dark. This is what makes the painting coexist with its surroundings.

The bluish tints are there because of the blue border. This again helps pull the painting together.

Materials List

SURFACE
This surface is available from Carolyn's Folk Art Studio, P.O. Box 624, Matthews, NC 38106. Phone (704) 847-0487.

WINSOR & NEWTON ARTISAN WATER MIXABLE OILS
- Lemon Yellow
- Yellow Ochre
- Raw Sienna
- Cadmium Red Light
- Permanent Alizarin Crimson
- Titanium White
- Ivory Black
- Prussian Blue

BRUSHES
- no. 4, no. 6 and no. 8 sable chisel blenders
- no. 1 round sable liner

ADDITIONAL SUPPLIES
- Delta Ceramcoat Blue Danube acrylic
- Delta Ceramcoat White acrylic
- ½-inch (1.3cm) sponge brush
- paper towels
- 220-grit wet/dry sandpaper
- Krylon Matte Finish spray no. 1311
- gold leaf adhesive
- gold leaf sheets
- piece of velvet or nylon hose
- Krylon Satin Varnish no. 1701
- odorless turpenoid
- oil palette
- dark graphite paper
- tracing paper
- ballpoint pen

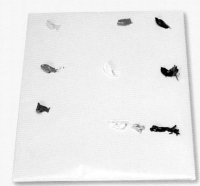

Leave the palette board white since your background is white.

Preparing the Background

Basecoat the tray following the preparation instructions in chapter two. Use White for the inset and Blue Danube for the decorative border. Transfer the pattern when dry.

What's Wrong With This Picture?

Even though yellow is a warm color, it will appear cool if it leans toward a greenish yellow. This lemon is too light and cool for its surroundings. It appears to be floating above the surface because the darks don't relate to the background. The lemon in the warm and colorful example relates better to its surroundings. It is warmer in temperature, consistent with the overall warmth of the painting, but it also has some cool tones to balance the warms and cools. The values are appropriate for the dark background and the shade color has some of the background color blended into it.

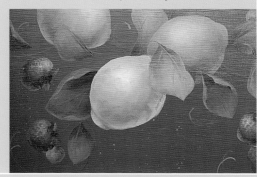

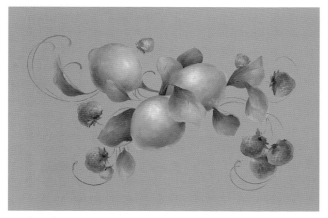

Warm and Colorful

This burgundy background is in great contrast to the yellow lemons. The Permanent Alizarin Crimson and Raw Sienna in the shadow area help the surface relate to the lemons. Using the background color in the shade area gives the illusion that the surface color is reflecting back up into the lemons, pulling the two elements together.

The leaves are warmer than in all the other paintings. This is because of the warmer temperature of the background—the use of warm tones in the leaves is consistent with the overall warm feeling of this painting. However, it is important to create both warms and cools in a painting. If I'm painting an overall warm painting then somewhere I want to introduce some cool tints. Notice the cooler shade area of the leaves. This was achieved by adding Permanent Alizarin Crimson, a cool red, to the green leaf mixtures.

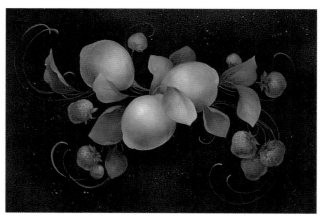

Cool and Neutral

This calm, restful mood is achieved by keeping the painting muted and close in value to the background. I used a cool background, cool leaves with warm tints, warm lemons with cool tints and incorporated the background color into the lemons.

Dark and Dramatic

These lemons are quite bright in the light area, but the shade area is close to the value of the background. The darkest darks in the leaves are as dark as the background. If the lemons on page 76 were put on a black background, they would appear to be floating above the surface.

Materials List *continued*

COLOR MIXES

LEMONS

Base
Lemon Yellow +
Titanium White

Shade
Lemon Yellow +
Raw Sienna

**Second Value
Shade**
Raw Sienna +
Ivory Black

Highlight
Titanium White

Reflected Light
Ivory Black +
Titanium White
+ a touch of
Prussian Blue

Accent
Cadmium Red
Light + Raw
Sienna

STRAWBERRIES

Base
Permanent
Alizarin Crimson
+ Cadmium Red
Light

Shade
Permanent
Alizarin Crimson
+ Ivory Black

Light
Base + a little
Lemon Yellow +
Titanium White

Highlight
Titanium White

Reflected Light
Ivory Black +
Titanium White
+ Prussian Blue

LEAVES

Base
Ivory Black +
Lemon Yellow +
Titanium White

Shade
Base + Ivory
Black

Highlight
Base + Titanium
White

Tints
Ivory Black +
Titanium White
+ Prussian Blue

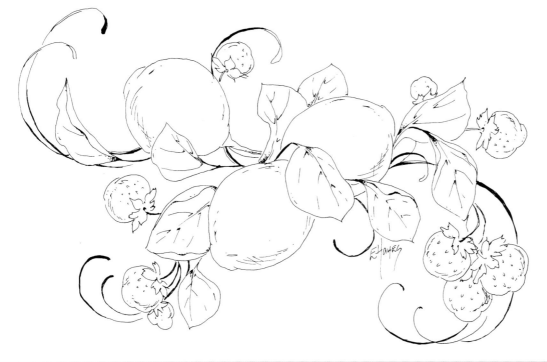

This pattern may
be hand-traced or
photocopied for
personal use only.
Enlarge 204% on
a photocopier to
return to full size.

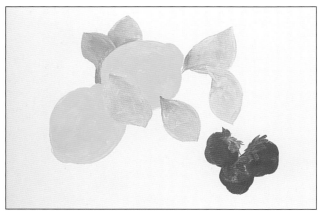

1 Base the lemons with Lemon Yellow plus a little Titanium White. Base the leaves with Ivory Black plus Lemon Yellow plus Titanium White in various temperatures and values. Base the strawberries with Permanent Alizarin Crimson plus Cadmium Red Light. Notice the green tones in the lemons; this comes from softly blending the elements together as described in project one. Spray dry this basecoat.

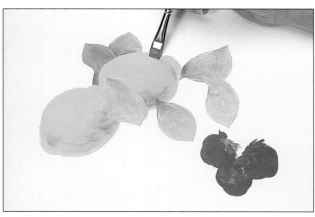

2 Place the shade on the lemons with Lemon Yellow and Raw Sienna. Fuzz this color out into the middle area.

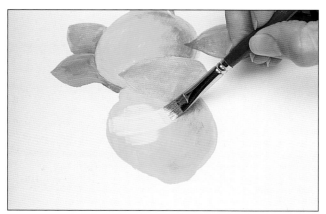

3 Place the highlight in a plus sign shape across the fattest part of the lemon using Lemon Yellow plus Titanium White. Make the horizontal bar longer. Follow the contour of the lemon. This will help convince the viewer that this lemon actually has dimension.

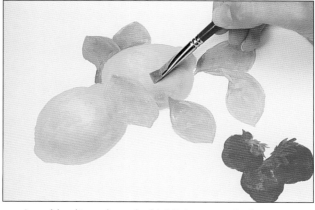

4 Start blending where the highlight meets the base. Use short, choppy strokes and wipe your brush often. Since I'm working on a dry basecoat, I sometimes pick up a little base color to help with the blending and transition between the light area and the dark area. When I'm through blending I've touched every area of the lemon with my brush.

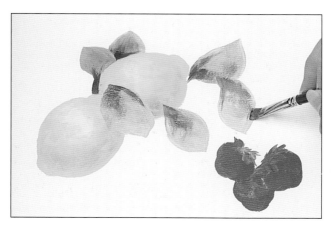

5 Place the shade in the most obvious dark area on the leaves, using the original base color plus a little more Ivory Black. Fuzz this color out.

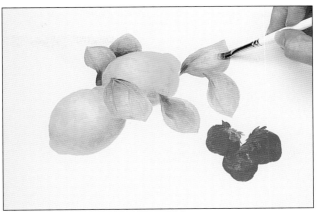

6 Highlight the leaves by adding Titanium White plus a little more Lemon Yellow to the base color. Add the stems and veins.

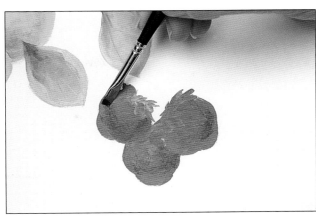

7 Place the shade on the strawberries in the most obvious dark area with Permanent Alizarin Crimson plus Ivory Black. Fuzz this color out into the middle area.

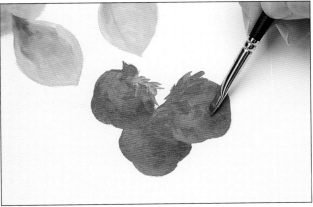

8 Place some base mix plus a little Lemon Yellow and Titanium White in the light area and blend out.

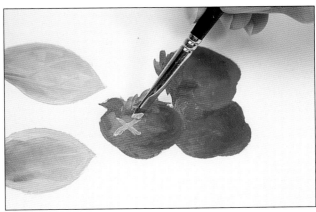

9 To create the texture of the strawberries, paint an **X** in the light area with Lemon Yellow plus Titanium White.

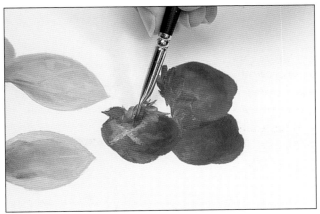

10 Using the corner of your chisel brush, soften the ends of the **X** as they move out from the highlight area.

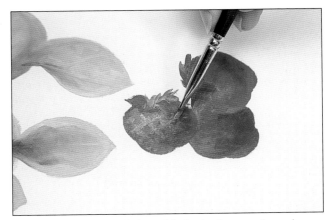

11 Create diamond-shaped holes in the strawberry by pressing the corner of your chisel brush into the wet paint. As you move away from the highlight area, these textured areas gradually diminish. If these areas become too intense in the middle or shade area, reapply Cadmium Red Light or Permanent Alizarin Crimson over the areas to soften them.

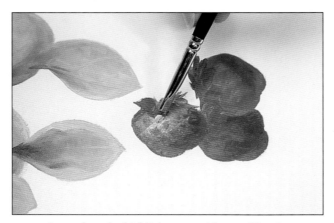

12 Strengthen the highlight area with pure Titanium White in the same manner as before.

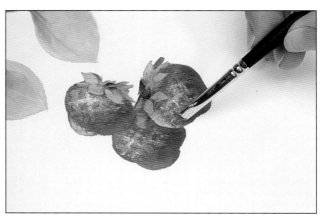

13 When I stand back and analyze my painting, I can see that my strawberries and leaves have more value change in them than the lemons do. Can you see the clean darks in the leaves and strawberries? I don't have any clean darks in the lemons. This has shifted the focal point to the strawberries and then the leaves. The other problem I see is that the lemons seem isolated because they don't have any colors from the strawberries in them. To help the strawberries relate to the leaves and lemons, place some yellow-greens from the leaf mixtures on the strawberries.

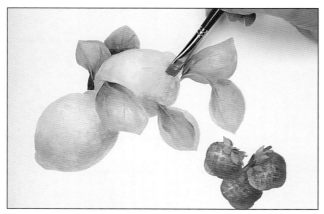

14 To fix the other areas of the painting, add some darker shade mixtures on the lemons using Raw Sienna plus Ivory Black in the most obvious dark areas. Next add some subtle red tones from the strawberries to the lemons to help pull those two elements together.

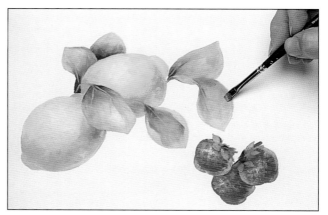

15 Place some reflected light on the lemons, strawberries and leaves with Ivory Black plus Titanium White plus Prussian Blue. I've purposely created a bluer mixture than I normally would to tie in with the blue frame. Once again, I'm trying to create a harmonious relationship between the painting and its background environment.

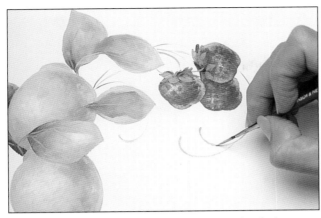

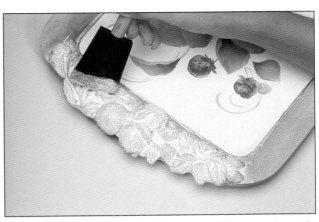

16 Thin down some light value greens with odorless turpenoid and use a liner brush to add your linework. Shade, lighten and accent the linework to give it more personality.

17 Thin down some Delta Ceramcoat White acrylic with water and brush on the raised portion of the tray, making sure you get the paint down into the crevices.

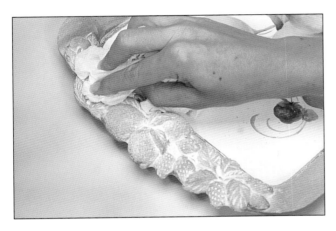

18 Immediately wipe off the white paint on the high areas with a soft cloth. This will create a white-washed look.

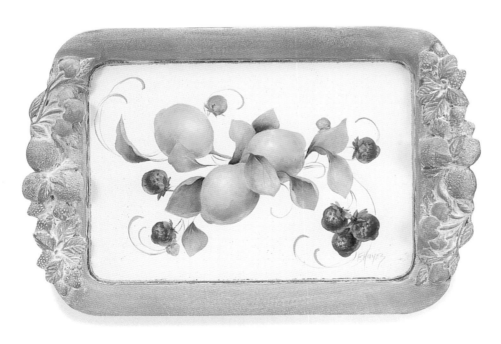

19 Spatter the tray with some light green leaf mixes. Varnish and enjoy.

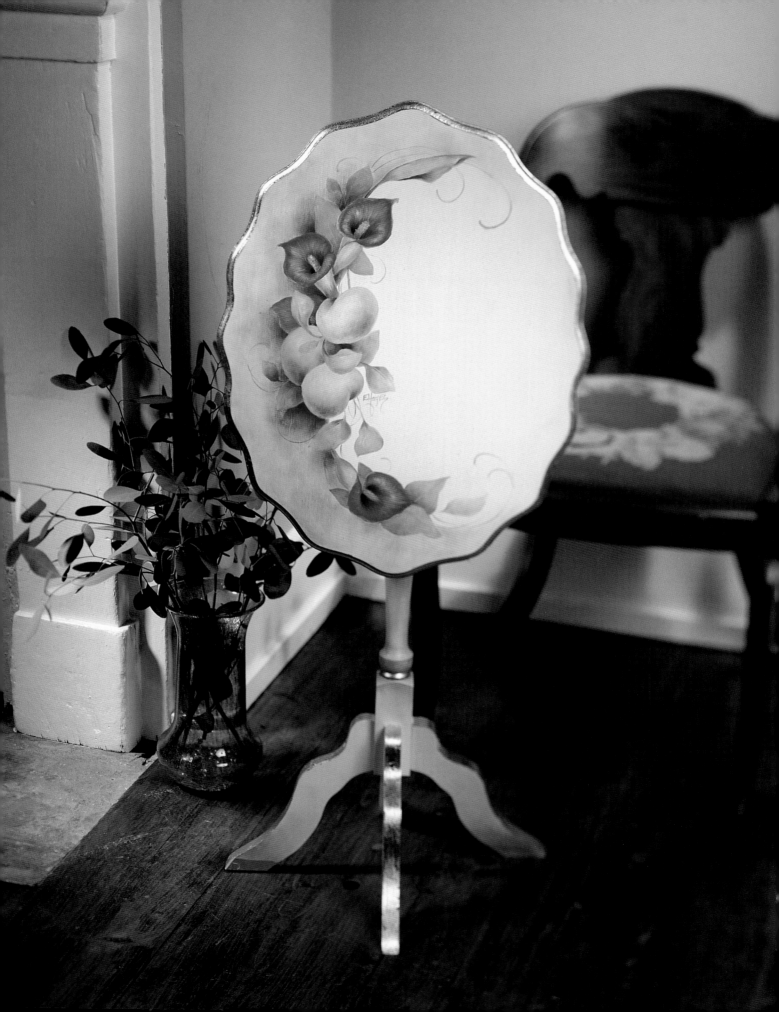

Peaches and Calla Lilies

THE FINISHING TOUCHES

Squiggle lines, rouging, gold leafing, antiquing and spattering can all add to the overall appeal of your painting. Consider them the accessories to a perfect outfit. The outfit might look great by itself, but with the right jewelry, it looks stunning.

Preparing the Background

Basecoat the table with Old Parchment acrylic following the instructions in chapter two. When dry, transfer the design.

⊰HINT⊱ *Inspiration comes from your surroundings. Look at colors, shapes and values around you. These all contribute to my inspiration when designing a new piece.*

For this piece my inspiration was the fabric I used to make curtains in my art studio. I loved the combination of yellows and cranberry tones, so I started there. I bought a wine-colored calla lily plant to sit in the windowsill and one day I was sitting at the window eating a peach and an idea was born. Look around you; there is inspiration everywhere.

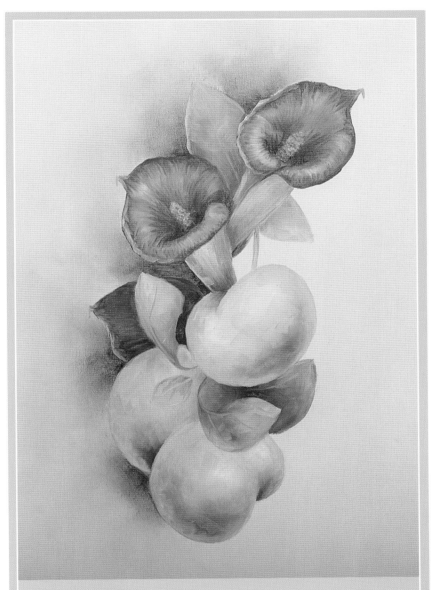

What's Wrong With This Picture?
This painting has no finishing touches—no linework, no spattering, no rouging. It looks plain and uninspiring. Always ask yourself, "What else can I do to make this painting better?"

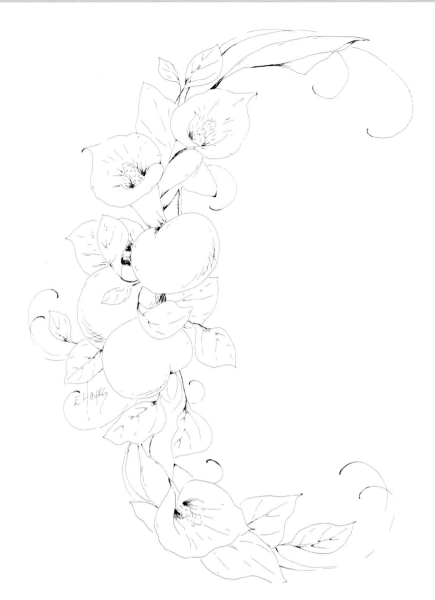

This pattern may be hand-traced or photocopied for personal use only. Enlarge 270% on a photocopier to return to full size.

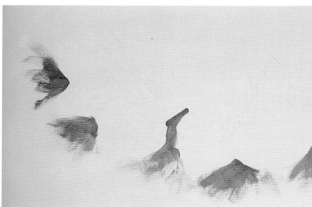

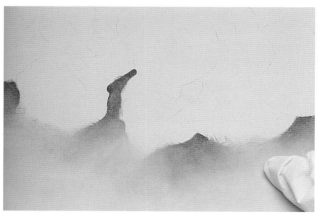

1 After tracing the pattern, place some Permanent Alizarin Crimson plus Ivory Black around the outside of the pattern. Keep this color dark and pure in the triangular areas and fuzz out away from the pattern. Do not use any medium.

2 With a soft cloth, use circular motions to soften the color. Keep the color stronger in the triangular areas near the pattern. If you want, you can spray dry at this point so that you won't get your hands into this rouging.

Materials List

COLOR MIXES

PEACHES

Base
Yellow Ochre +
Lemon Yellow +
Titanium White

Shade
Permanent
Alizarin Crimson
+ Raw Sienna +
a little Ivory
Black

Light
Base + Lemon
Yellow +
Titanium White

Highlight
Titanium White

LEAVES

Base
Ivory Black +
Lemon Yellow +
Titanium White

Shade
Base + Ivory
Black

Light
Lemon Yellow +
Titanium White

CALLA LILIES

Base
Permanent
Alizarin Crimson
+ Raw Sienna

Shade
Permanent
Alizarin Crimson
+ Ivory Black

Light
Yellow Ochre +
a little Lemon
Yellow +
Titanium White

Reflected Light
Ivory Black +
Titanium White

SURFACE

This tilt-top table is available from Wayne's Woodenware, 1913 State Road 150, Neenah, WI 54956. Phone (800) 840-1497, fax (920) 725-9386 or E-mail Waynes@vbe.com.

WINSOR & NEWTON ARTISAN WATER MIXABLE OILS

- Lemon Yellow
- Yellow Ochre
- Raw Sienna
- Permanent Alizarin Crimson
- Titanium White
- Ivory Black

BRUSHES

- no. 6, no. 8 and no. 10 sable chisel blenders
- no. 1 round sable liner

ADDITIONAL SUPPLIES

- Delta Ceramcoat Old Parchment acrylic
- Delta Ceramcoat Red Iron Oxide acrylic
- 1-inch (2.5cm) sponge brush
- paper towels
- 220-grit wet/dry sandpaper
- Krylon Matte Finish spray no. 1311
- odorless turpenoid
- oil palette
- dark graphite paper

- tracing paper
- ballpoint pen
- soft cloth
- gold leaf adhesive
- gold leaf sheets
- bristle brush
- piece of velvet or nylon hose
- Krylon Satin Varnish no. 1701

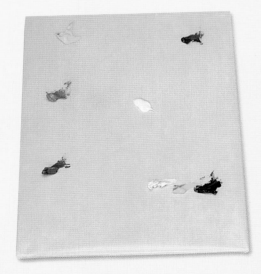

Basecoat the palette board with Old Parchment acrylic.

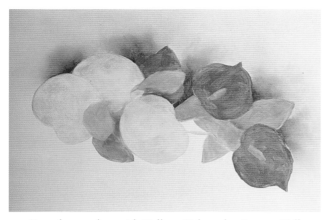

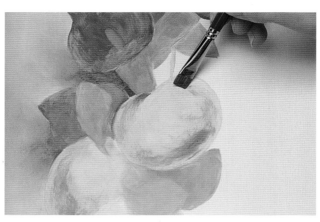

3 Base the peaches with Yellow Ochre plus Lemon Yellow plus Titanium White. Base the "face" of the calla lily with Permanent Alizarin Crimson plus a little Raw Sienna. Base the stamen with Yellow Ochre. Base the leaves and stem area of the calla lilies using various temperatures and values of Ivory Black plus Lemon Yellow plus Titanium White. Soften any hard edges between elements to create an out-of-focus look. Spray dry.

4 Shade the peaches with Permanent Alizarin Crimson plus Raw Sienna plus a little Ivory Black in the darkest areas. Place this color in the most obvious dark areas and fuzz out.

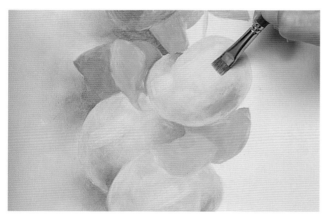

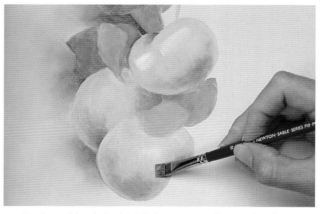

5 Highlight using the base color plus more Lemon Yellow plus Titanium White. Place this color across the fat part of the peach.

6 Begin to blend the highlight out into the peach. If necessary, pick up a little original base color to help with the blending. Add more Lemon Yellow plus Titanium White to your highlight mix and bring the highlight up one more step.

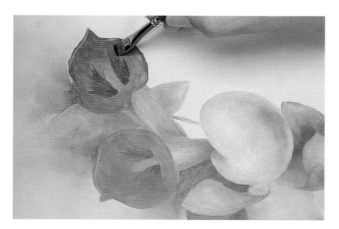

7 Here I've shaded and highlighted the leaves using colors from the ribbon of greens. Place the shade on the calla lilies in the most obvious dark areas with Permanent Alizarin Crimson plus Ivory Black. Keep the color clean and pure at the point where the throat of the lily and the front area wraps around. Fuzz the color up.

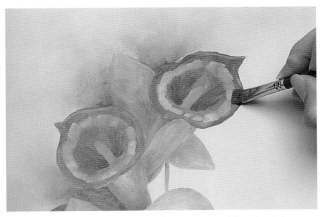

8 Reapply a small amount of Permanent Alizarin Crimson on the dried basecoat in the highlight area. Using the peach base color, place the highlight on the lily. Try to visualize how this lily is formed and how the light would hit the areas that are closest to you.

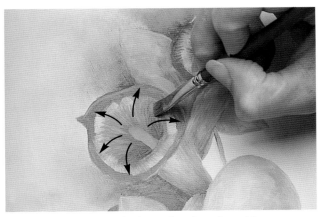

9 Using the chisel end of your brush and working on one side of the highlight, chisel back and forth between the highlight and the basecoat. Follow the contour of the lily by pulling into the throat and gently arching out. Dry wipe your brush whenever you feel that you've picked up too much paint on your brush.

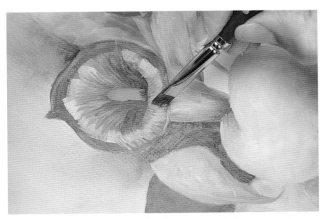

10 When you come to the front area of the lily, make sure you stay within the front petal area. Don't chisel into the dark throat area. Chisel the other side of the highlight as before. Remember to follow the contour of the lily.

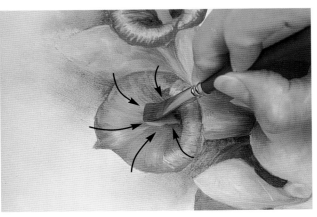

11 Dry wipe your brush and place it on the outside edge of the lily. Very softly, pull down following the contour. Dry wipe again and continue softening the highlight. Dry wipe between each stroke.

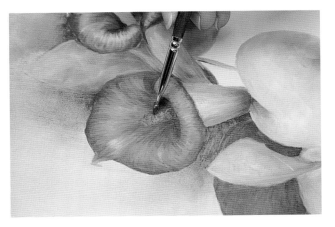

12 Shade the stamen with Permanent Alizarin Crimson plus Raw Sienna. Place this color on very splotchy using the corner of your chisel brush.

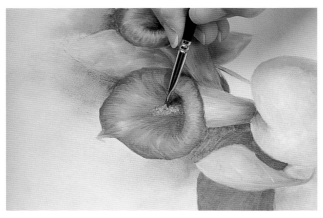

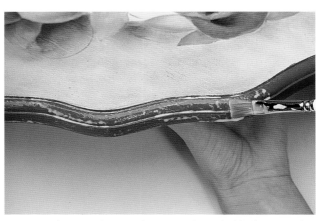

13 Lighten the stamen with Yellow Ochre plus Lemon Yellow plus Titanium White, using the same method. Place a cool reflected light on with a mix of Ivory Black and Titanium White. This color helps cool down an otherwise very warm painting (see page 91 for placement).

14 Make sure the wood is properly sealed before you do any gold leafing. If it hasn't been sealed, the sizing will soak into the wood and the leafing won't stick. Apply a red basecoat under all the areas that will have the leafing. I use Delta Ceramcoat Red Iron Oxide. Apply the sizing with an old brush. Don't use your good oil brushes; it will ruin them. The sizing goes on milky and dries clear. When it is clear, it's time to add the leafing.

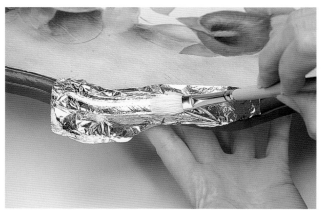

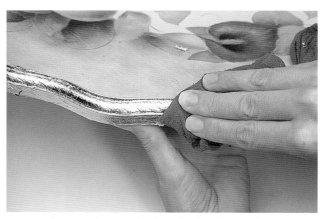

15 The gold leaf sheets are very thin and have a tendency to soak up the oils on your fingers. To avoid fingerprints, wash your hands thoroughly before handling the leaf, wear painter's gloves or lightly rub baby powder on your hands. Carefully tear away a section of leaf that will be easy to work with. Try to handle the leaf as little as possible. Apply it to the sizing and smooth it down using a bristle brush.

16 After you have applied the leaf and smoothed it down, take a piece of velvet or nylon hose and begin buffing. The more you rub, the shinier the leaf will be.

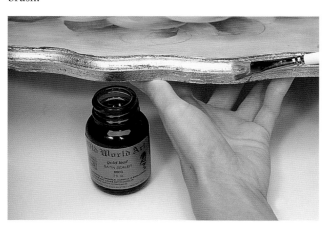

17 Last, apply a sealer. This will keep the leaf from tarnishing and keep it shiny. The wonderful thing about leafing is the cracks and tears that form, allowing the red basecoat to come through.

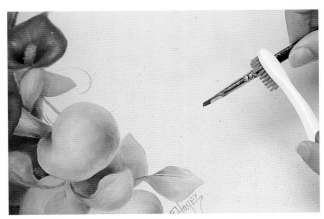

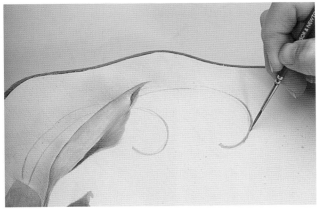

18 Spattering softens the background and adds another interesting element to the design. Thin down colors from your palette with odorless turpenoid; for this piece I've chosen yellow tones from the peaches. Take an old toothbrush and brush it into the thinned down paint. Next, drag the toothbrush over the handle of another brush. Move the toothbrush around the design as you do this. Add as much or as little spattering as you like, but don't make it so noticeable that it detracts from the painting.

19 Linework helps pull the eye through the design. Don't trace any pattern lines for the linework; your hand will shake as you try to stay within the line. Spray dry the surface before you add the linework; if you don't like what you paint, you can wipe it off easily with a kneaded eraser. I generally use greens from my palette for my linework. Thin down a value that is appropriate for the background you are working on: a light green for a light background and a dark green for a dark background. Keep your hand loose and visualize where you want the linework to go. Always pull the lines toward you. After the initial linework has been painted, come back and add some darks, lights and accents to the lines.

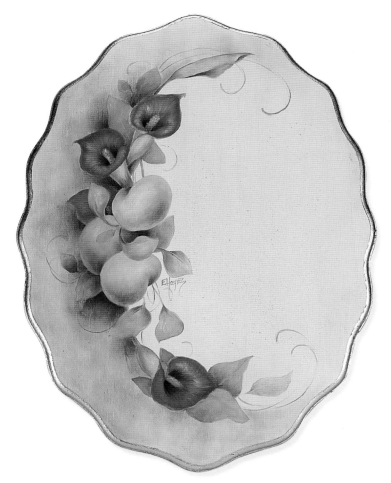

20 Antique the legs and stand using the same color and technique described on page 86. See page 84 for placement. Gold leaf the accent turns on the stand and a 1 inch (2.5cm) band on the bottom of the feet. Varnish.

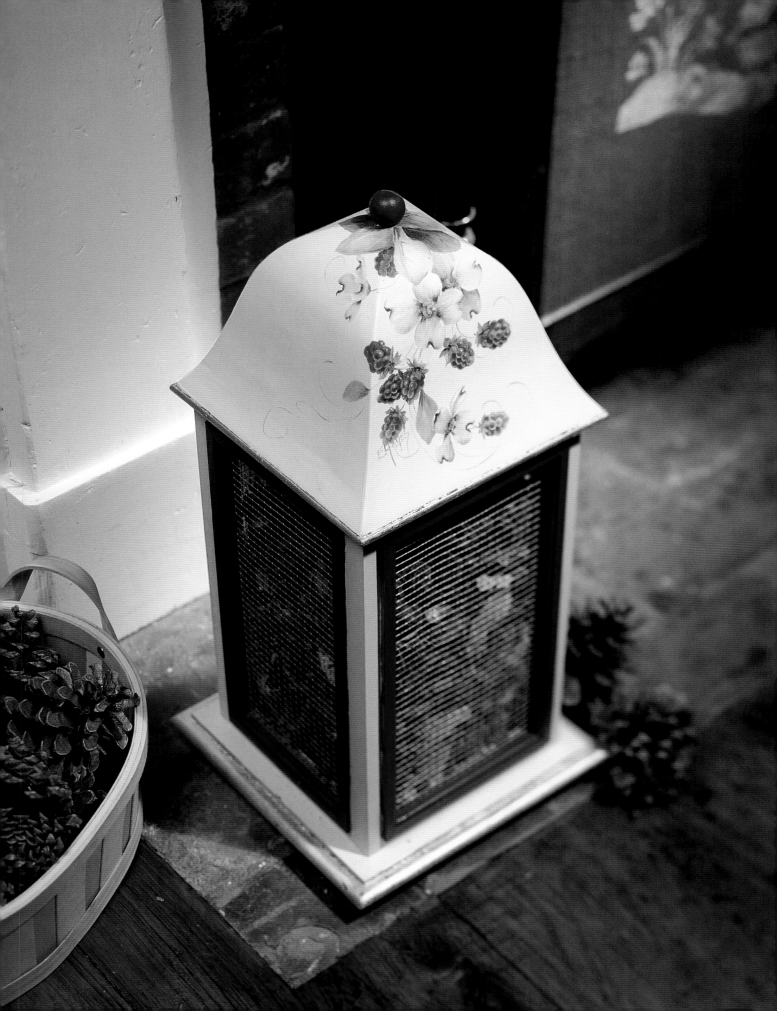

Raspberries and Dogwood

CONSIDERING A LIGHT SOURCE

When painting a decorative piece that isn't in the form of a traditional still life, I don't confine myself with the laws of light that would determine cast shadows. Instead, I imagine my designs growing on a branch with the sun glistening on the elements as they sway in a gentle breeze.

On this piece, the light on the raspberries appears to be coming from up above and the highlights are on the top side of the raspberries. If this were a still life, the highlights would be more regimented and there would be cast shadows.

Try to think of movement as you paint and your paintings will appear to be alive.

Preparing the Background

Basecoat the potpourri box with a mix of Delta Ceramcoat Dresden Flesh plus Jo Sonja's All Purpose Sealer following the instructions on pages 10-11. Paint the top knob, feet and trim with Delta Ceramcoat Black Cherry. Transfer the design.

Creating Your Own Designs

Creating your own designs is another step in your progress as a decorative artist. I can remember when I didn't have the foggiest idea how to begin designing an original pattern. Just like everything else, take it step by step. Here are some basic principles that can get you started.

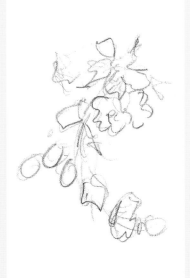

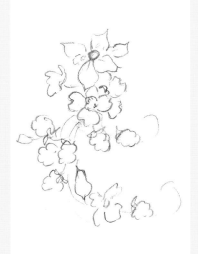

First, choose a letter shape for your design to follow—C, S, L or O. If you look at my designs, you will notice they are all in the shape of one of these letters. The raspberries and dogwoods project is a C-shape. Draw a thumbnail sketch (a small, quick sketch) of your design. Don't try to draw a full-scale design right from the start. My thumbnail sketches are basically just scribbles.

Gradually begin to refine the shapes, such as the fruit and leaves. Finally, refine the idea to scale, making it the appropriate size for your surface.

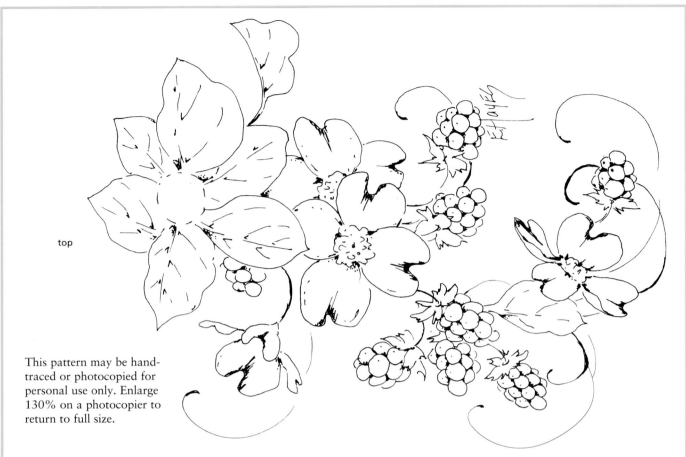

top

This pattern may be hand-traced or photocopied for personal use only. Enlarge 130% on a photocopier to return to full size.

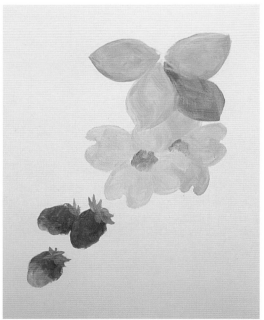

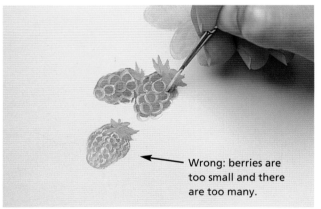

Wrong: berries are too small and there are too many.

1 Basecoat the raspberries with Permanent Alizarin Crimson. Base the dogwoods with Titanium White plus Yellow Ochre plus Ivory Black. Base the leaves in various values and temperatures of Ivory Black plus Lemon Yellow plus Titanium White. Paint the center of the dogwoods with the same green mixtures and add a little light yellow-green to the tip of the bottom raspberry.

2 Begin to outline the individual berries with Titanium White and a liner brush. Don't be afraid to go outside the basecoat with this outline and don't make the berries too tiny.

Materials List

COLOR MIXES

RASPBERRIES

Base	**Shade**	**Light**	**Highlight**	**Tints + Reflected Light**
Permanent Alizarin Crimson	Permanent Alizarin Crimson + Ivory Black	Cadmium Red Light + Titanium White	Titanium White	greens from leaves

DOGWOODS

Base	**Shade**	**Accent**	**Light**	**Highlight**
Titanium White + Yellow Ochre + Ivory Black	Base + Permanent Alizarin Crimson + Ivory Black	Permanent Alizarin Crimson + Ivory Black	Base + Lemon Yellow + Titanium White	Titanium White

LEAVES

Base	**Shade**	**Light**
Ivory Black + Lemon Yellow + Titanium White	Base + Ivory Black	Base + Titanium White

DARKER LEAVES

Base	**Shade**	**Light**
Ivory Black + Lemon Yellow + Titanium White	Base + Ivory Black + Permanent Alizarin Crimson	Base + Titanium White

SURFACE

This surface is available from PCM Studios, 731 Highland Avenue, Suite D, Atlanta, GA 30312. Phone (404) 222-0348 or E-mail abjpcm@aol.com.

WINSOR & NEWTON ARTISAN WATER MIXABLE OILS

- Lemon Yellow
- Yellow Ochre
- Raw Sienna
- Cadmium Red Light
- Permanent Alizarin Crimson
- Titanium White
- Ivory Black

BRUSHES

- no. 2, no. 4 and no. 6 sable chisel blenders
- no. 1 round sable liner

ADDITIONAL SUPPLIES

- Delta Ceramcoat Dresden Flesh acrylic
- Delta Ceramcoat Black Cherry acrylic
- ½-inch (1.3cm) sponge brush
- paper towels
- 220-grit wet/dry sandpaper
- Krylon Matte Finish spray no. 1311
- gold leaf adhesive
- gold leaf sheets
- piece of velvet or nylon hose
- Krylon Satin Varnish no. 1701
- odorless turpenoid
- oil palette
- dark graphite paper
- tracing paper
- ballpoint pen

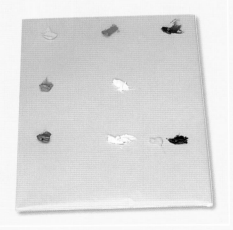

Basecoat the palette board with Dresden Flesh acrylic.

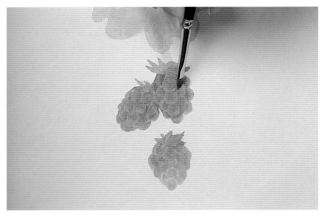

3 With a small flat brush, soften the outline by blending the Titanium White into each individual berry. Spray dry.

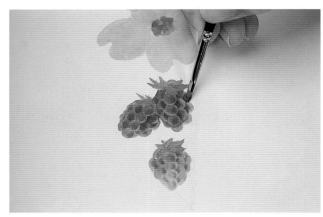

4 Shade using Permanent Alizarin Crimson plus a little Ivory Black. Place a crescent-shaped shadow on the right side of the main row of berries. Shade the the triangular areas of the berries that gradually move away from you.

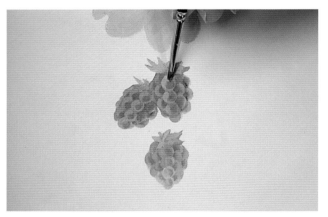

5 Place some light on the lefthand side of the berry with Cadmium Red Light plus Titanium White. The main row of berries should be lightest; as each row gradually moves away the light should diminish.

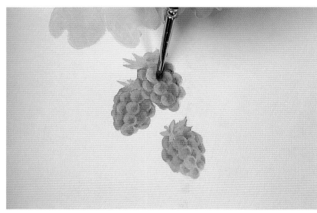

6 Blend the light area.

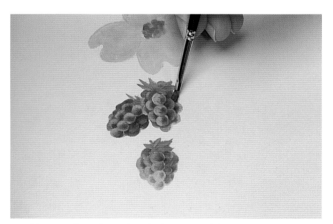

7 Deepen the triangular dark areas with more Permanent Alizarin Crimson plus Ivory Black.

⁂HINT⁂ Organize your painting area and play inspiring music while you work. I've painted my art room a sunny yellow with white cabinets that brings a smile to my face every time I walk in the room. You'll paint better and enjoy yourself more if you're comfortable and happy in your environment.

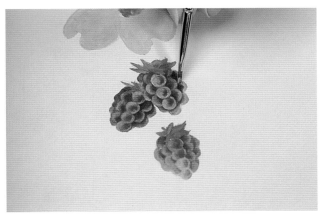

8 Place some reflected light on the right side of the raspberry with a light yellow-green from the leaves. This color also acts as a tint and helps the raspberries relate to the leaves.

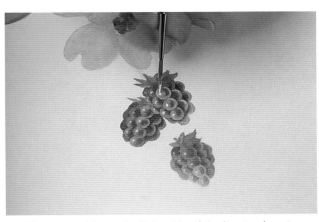

9 Place a sparkle on the light side of the berries, keeping the color brighter and cleaner on the main row with pure Titanium White. Don't blend this out. As each row moves away from you, the sparkle should diminish slightly.

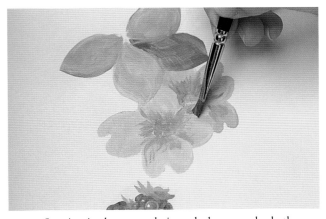

10 Starting in the most obvious dark areas, shade the dogwoods with the base color plus Permanent Alizarin Crimson plus a little Ivory Black. Fuzz this color up into the flower.

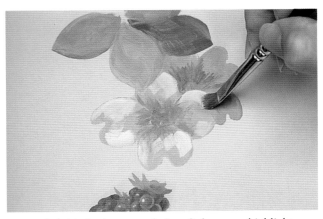

11 Starting in the most obvious light areas, highlight using the base color plus a little Lemon Yellow plus Titanium White. This mixture is quite a bit thicker than my shade color since I'm using more opaque paint.

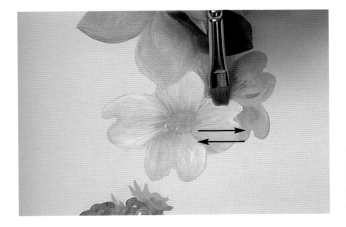

12 Pick up a little base color and use the chisel edge of your brush to chisel back and forth between the shade and highlight colors. Dry wipe your brush anytime you feel you've picked up too much paint. The streakiness created by the chisel creates the illusion of veins running through the petal. If the streaks get too obvious, soften them by brushing over them with a dry wiped brush.

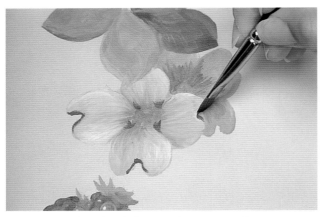

13 Strengthen the darks near the center with Permanent Alizarin Crimson plus Ivory Black. Using this color, place accents on the tips of the petals.

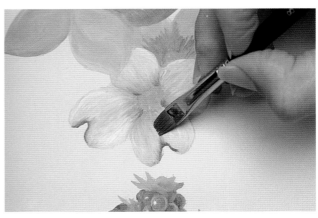

14 Using a dry wiped brush and the chisel end of your brush, gently chisel this dark accent color into the wet paint. Don't overblend this area; you want the color clean and strong on the outside edge.

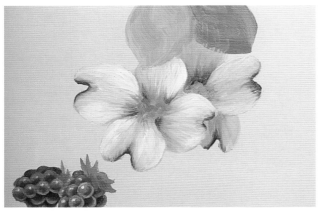

15 Lighten the top dogwood by adding more Titanium White. Keep the underneath dogwood darker and duller.

What's Wrong With This Picture?
The light source on these berries is too confusing. It's coming from two different directions. Even though I don't confine myself to a "still life" light source, I still want to keep the lights consistent, especially when painting a cluster of berries.

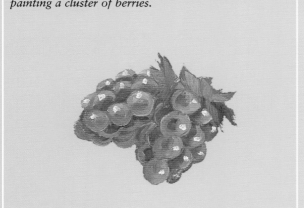

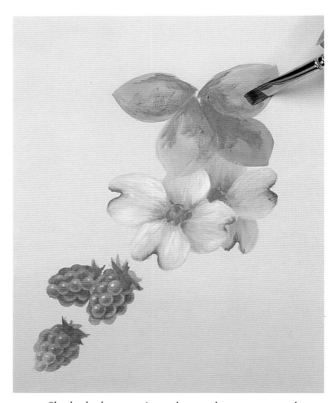

16 Shade the leaves using values and temperatures that are appropriate for each leaf. Keep the color thin and fuzzy. Shade the flower center by adding a darker green mix. Keep this color choppy.

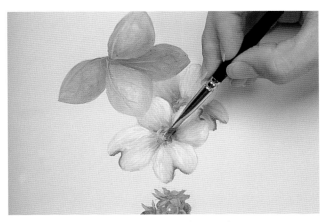

17 Highlight the leaves using values and temperatures that are appropriate for each leaf. Highlight the flower center by adding a lighter green. Keep the center choppy; this gives the illusion of texture.

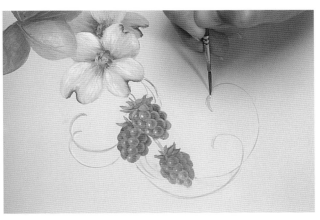

18 Add scrollwork with light green mixtures thinned with odorless turpenoid. Shade, lighten and accent the scrollwork.

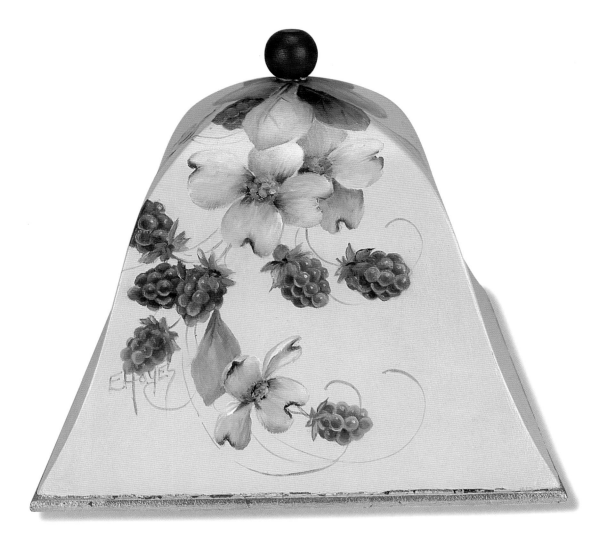

19 To finish this piece, gold leaf the rim on the top and the trim at the bottom following gold leafing instructions on page 91. Varnish, fill with potpourri and enjoy.

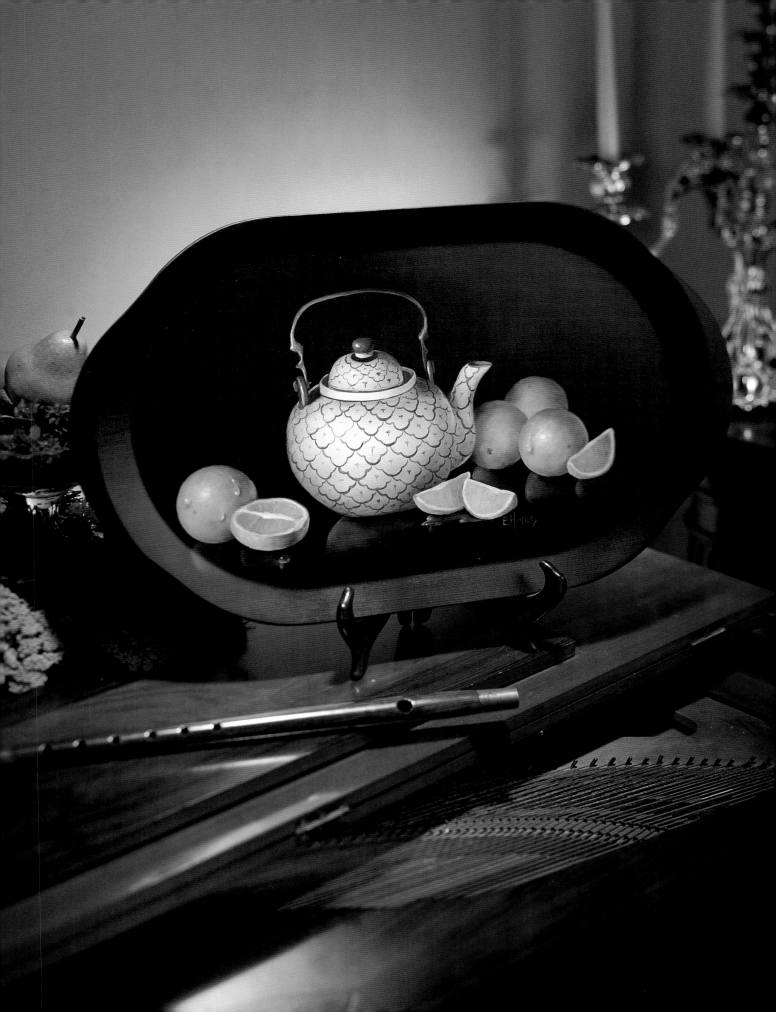

Orange Tea

LOST AND FOUND AREAS

A found area is one that has crisp, defined edges and draws our attention. A lost area is one that gets little attention; its soft edges often fade into the background.

Years ago, a woman commented on how much my painting looked like decals. I think she meant it as a compliment, but I was mortified. I realized at that point that my painting did have a cut-and-paste look. All of the elements in my painting had hard, found edges. There were no lost areas.

It's hard to create lost areas. Let's face it, we want everyone to notice every little detail of our painting, but some details are better left unsaid.

Think of an orchestra—the first string violinists are the ones that get our attention; we hear them loudest. We don't hear the third string violinists or notice them quite as much as the first string; but nonetheless, they are there to support the first string. In the grand scheme of things, they are just as important.

Preparing the Background

Basecoat the tray with Black acrylic following the instructions in chapter two. Transfer the design when dry.

What's Wrong With This Picture?
See how the front orange slice jumps out at you? The rind area is too sharp and all the edges are very crisp and hard; the rind doesn't even look like it belongs to the orange. There are no lost areas within the orange. In addition, there is a strong, dark outline between the two oranges. This makes the orange stiff and hard to look at. Finally, the outside edges of the oranges are too light for the black background. They don't appear to be moving away from us. Everything is found and nothing is lost. A good painting consists of both lost and found areas.

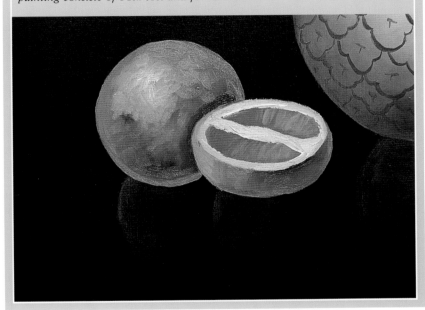

⁂HINT ⁂ *The use of complementary color is always striking. Complements are colors that are opposite each other on the color wheel. Yellow is the complement to violet, green is the complement to red and orange is the complement to blue.*

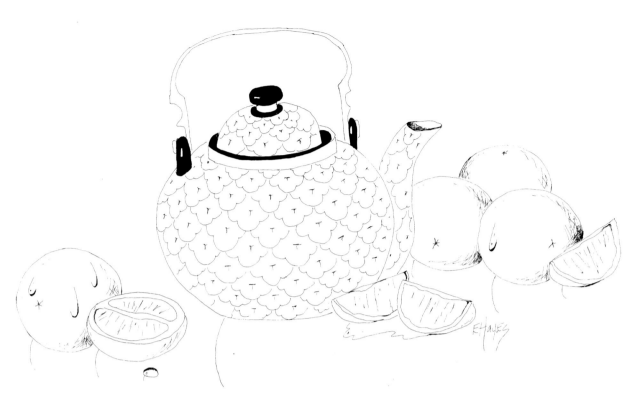

This pattern may be hand-traced or photocopied for personal use only. Enlarge 213% on a photocopier to return to full size.

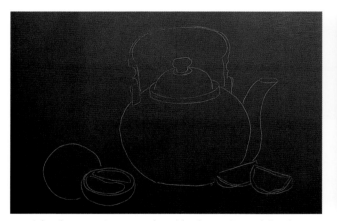

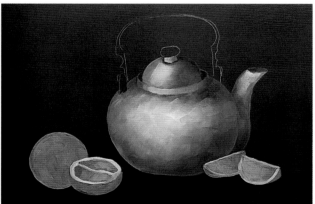

1 After basecoating, transfer only the outline of the design. Do not transfer the detailing on the teapot.

2 Block in the teapot from dark to light using the mixes on page 103. Concentrate on following the contour of the teapot and developing a sense of roundness. Base in the oranges with Cadmium Orange plus Yellow Ochre. Use Yellow Ochre plus Titanium White for the rind area.

Materials List

COLOR MIXES

ORANGES

Base	**Shade**	**Second Value Shade**	**Light**	**Highlight**	**Reflected Light**
Cadmium Orange + Yellow Ochre	Base + Ivory Black	Shade + Prussian Blue	Cadmium Orange	Cadmium Orange + Lemon Yellow + Titanium White	Ivory Black + Titanium White + French Ultramarine Blue

TEAPOT

Darkest Value	**Second Darkest Value**	**Midvalue**	**Second Lightest Value**	**Lightest Value**	**Detailing**
Burnt Umber + Ivory Black + Prussian Blue	Burnt Umber + Ivory Black	Second Darkest Value + Raw Sienna + Titanium White	Midvalue + Yellow Ochre + Titanium White	Second Lightest Value + Titanium White	French Ultramarine Blue

HANDLE

Base	**Shade**	**Light**	**Highlight**
Raw Sienna	Ivory Black + Raw Sienna + Prussian Blue	Yellow Ochre	Lemon Yellow + Titanium White

SURFACE

This surface is available from Carolyn's Folk Art Studio, P.O. Box 624, Matthews NC 38106. Phone (704) 847-0487.

WINSOR & NEWTON ARTISAN WATER MIXABLE OILS

- Lemon Yellow
- Cadmium Orange
- Yellow Ochre
- Raw Sienna
- Burnt Umber
- Permanent Alizarin Crimson
- Prussian Blue
- French Ultramarine Blue
- Titanium White
- Ivory Black

BRUSHES

- no. 4, no. 6, no. 8 and no. 10 sable chisel blenders
- no. 1 round sable liner

ADDITIONAL SUPPLIES

- Delta Ceramcoat Black acrylic
- 1-inch (2.5cm) sponge brush
- paper towels

- 220-grit wet/dry sandpaper
- Krylon Matte Finish spray no. 1311
- Krylon Satin Varnish no. 1701
- odorless turpenoid
- Winsor & Newton Blending and Glazing Medium
- oil palette
- light graphite paper
- tracing paper
- ballpoint pen

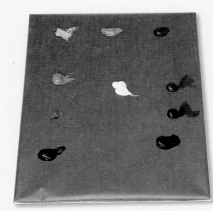

Basecoat the palette board with Black acrylic.

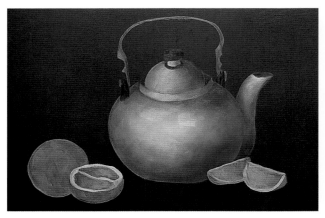

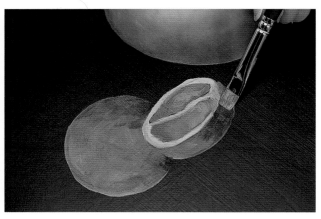

3 Refine the blending on the teapot. Paint the handle with Raw Sienna. Paint the top knob and side handles with French Ultramarine Blue. Spray dry.

4 Shade the orange using the base color plus a little Ivory Black. Place this color in the most obvious dark areas and fuzz out. Adding a little Prussian Blue to this shade mix and placing it in the core dark areas will create a stronger dark that will help the orange relate to the black background.

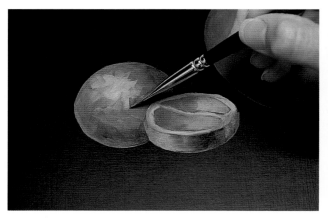

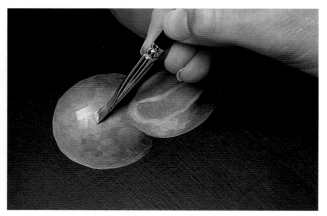

5 Lighten the orange gradually by adding Cadmium Orange in the light area.

6 Continue to highlight the orange by adding Cadmium Orange plus Lemon Yellow plus a little Titanium White.

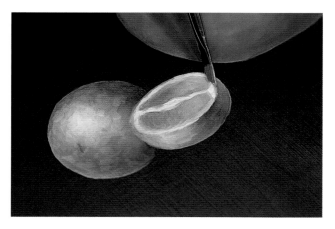

7 Lighten the rind by adding a small amount of Lemon Yellow and Titanium White to the base color. Remember to create lost and found edges.

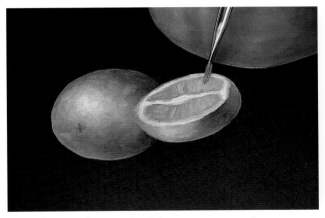

8 Following the growth of the orange, create the suggestion of the pulp in the orange slice by adding some Cadmium Orange with the chisel end of your brush. Be careful not to create stripes.

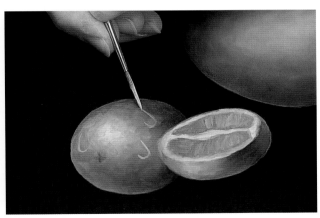

9 Using a liner brush, outline the water drop with a little Lemon Yellow and Titanium White.

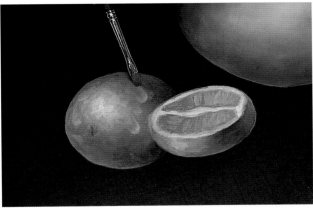

10 Using a small flat brush, soften the outline by blending the outline into the inside of the water drop.

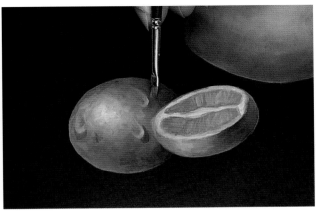

11 Place a shadow under the water drop with a value darker than what it is resting upon.

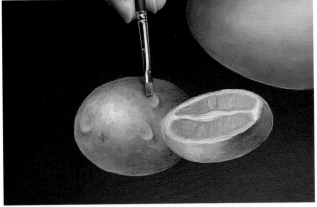

12 Soften the entire water drop so that there are no hard edges. It should be very hazy at this stage.

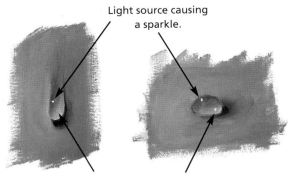

Light source causing a sparkle.

The light passes through the drop, lighting the opposite side.

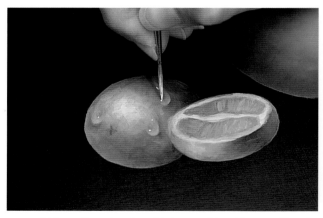

13 Using a liner brush, add the sparkle with pure Titanium White. Don't blend this out.

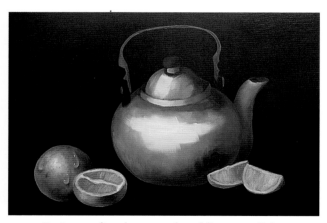

14 Begin to refine the teapot by adding more light tones in the light area. Concentrate on keeping the shape of the teapot rounded. To help blend, pick up some of the original base color.

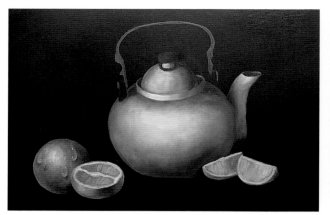

15 Before going any farther, I want to analyze what I've done so far. My teapot and oranges have nice darks and lights, lost and founds, and the placement of values gives the illusion of dimension.

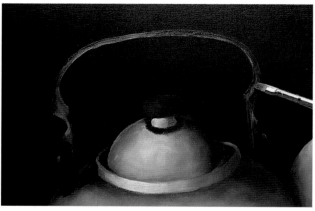

16 Add some lighter tones on the handle with Yellow Ochre and some darker tones with Ivory Black plus Raw Sienna plus Prussian Blue. Make some edges of the handle very dark so that they disappear into the background color.

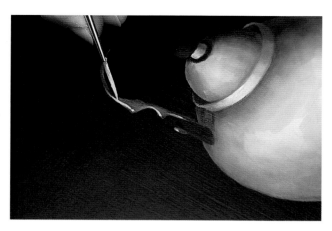

17 The trick to painting brass and other shiny metals is to create a lot of contrast in values. Here I've place a strong shine area with Lemon Yellow plus Titanium White. Don't blend this out. Keep it clean and pure.

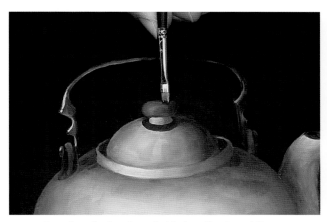

18 Develop the knob and side handles by adding some light areas with French Ultramarine Blue plus Titanium White. Notice how dark the dark side of the knob is. This is a lost area. To lose an edge on a dark background, make it very dark. To lose an edge on a light background, make it very light.

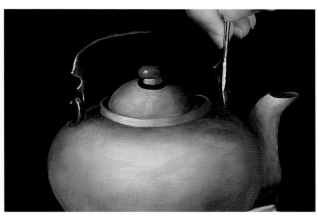

19 Place the shine on the knob and handles with a liner brush and Titanium White. Carefully soften the outside edges of the highlight, keeping the color clean and pure in the center. Spray dry before applying the detailing to the pot.

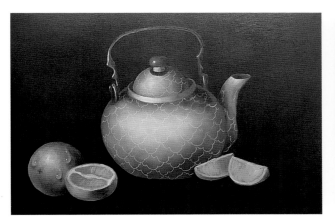

20 After spray drying, apply the detail pattern on the teapot with graphite paper. Make sure the spray is thoroughly dry before you apply the pattern.

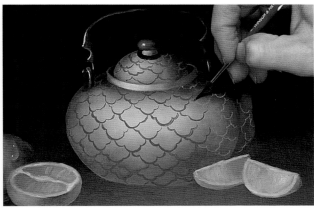

21 Using a liner brush, thin French Ultramarine Blue with glazing medium. If you are using water mixable oils, use the medium specially formulated for these paints. Carefully follow the pattern and apply the detailing on the pot.

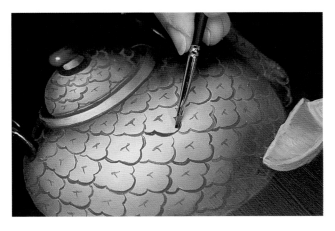

22 Clean up any overly heavy lines or erase any pattern lines that show with a clean brush and turpenoid. When the detailing is finished, spray dry.

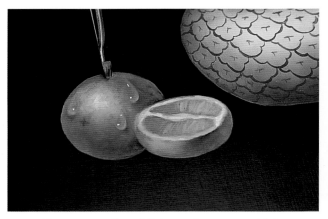

23 Place some reflected light on the orange with Ivory Black plus Titanium White plus French Ultramarine Blue. Keep this color thin and splotchy.

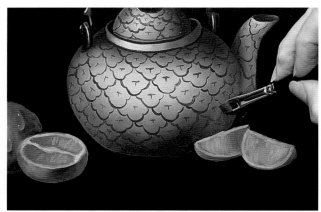

24 Add some orange reflections on the teapot with Cadmium Orange plus Yellow Ochre, using a dry brush. This is the wonderful advantage to spray drying—I can add these reflections without messing up what I've already painted.

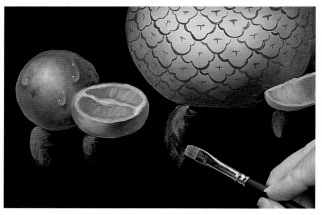

25 Place some reflections on the surface using Cadmium Orange plus Yellow Ochre for the oranges and Yellow Ochre plus a little Titanium White for the teapot.

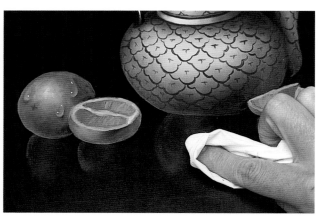

26 Using a soft cloth, soften the reflection so that it gradually disappears into the surface.

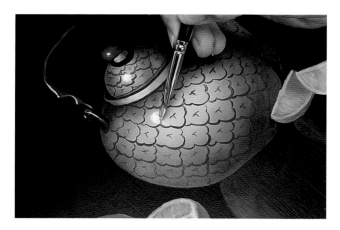

27 Place a shine spot on the teapot with pure Titanium White.

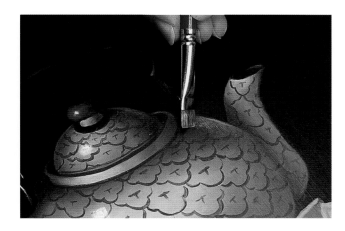

28 Add some reflected light to the teapot using Ivory Black, Titanium White and French Ultramarine Blue.

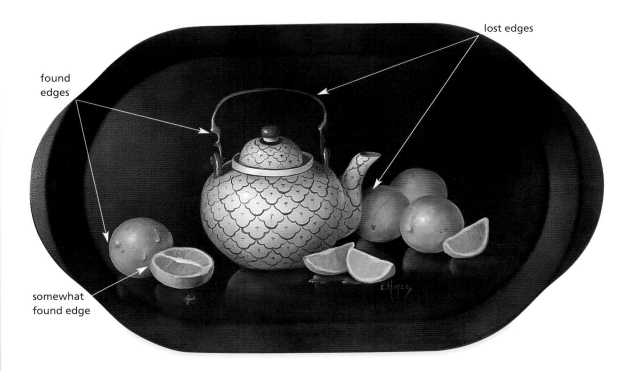

found edges

lost edges

somewhat found edge

29 I'd have to say that this was my favorite piece to paint. I love the combination of complementary colors and painting on a dark background. This painting makes good use of lost and found areas. There are areas of the oranges and teapot that are fading into the dark background and there are strong found areas that draw your eye. There are also cool tints on the warm oranges and warm tints on the cool teapot. A good learning experience would be to paint this on a light background and see how it would affect the way you handle the lost and found edges.

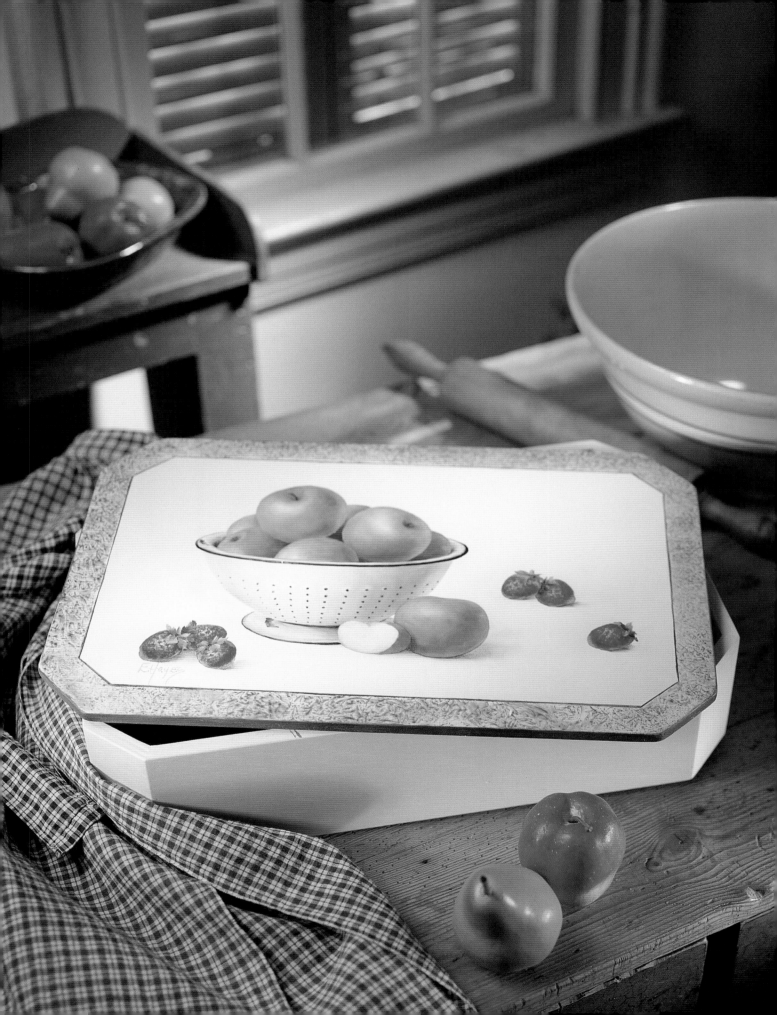

Apples in a Colander

THE ALL-IMPORTANT HIGHLIGHT

When painting round objects, think spherically. Light will hit the area that is closest to it. As the object moves away from the light, the color diminishes.

Sometimes, as decorative artists, we get so familiar with the traditional guidelines "shadows fall in the form of a crescent" and "objects in the back need to be darker" that we fail to notice how light reacts on an actual object.

Sometimes, as in this still life, an element can be in the farthest plane and still be lighter than what is in front of it.

These apples and strawberries are in the form of a sphere, however, the area that the stems grow from is wider and thicker than the blossom end. This dictates that the light will travel across this thick part of the apple. The light that is reflected by the other apples affects the shadow side of the apple. Set up your own still life with fruit and

see how the light affects each object.

Preparing the Background

Basecoat the surface using Raw Linen, following the instructions in chapter two. Transfer only the outside pattern lines. Don't transfer the holes in the colander.

What's Wrong With This Picture?

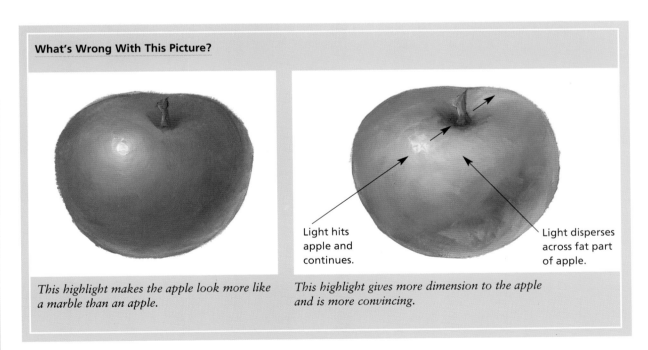

Light hits apple and continues.

Light disperses across fat part of apple.

This highlight makes the apple look more like a marble than an apple.

This highlight gives more dimension to the apple and is more convincing.

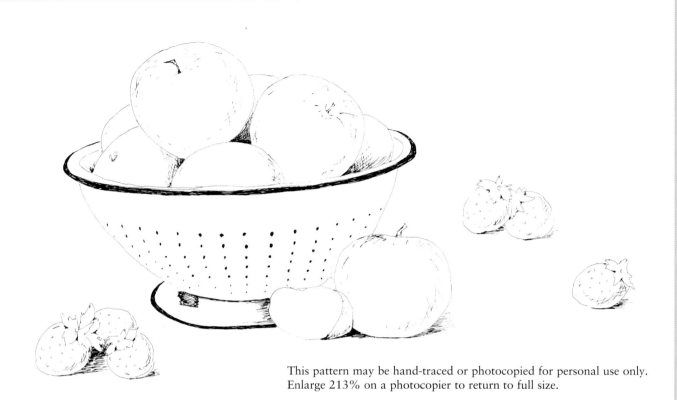

This pattern may be hand-traced or photocopied for personal use only. Enlarge 213% on a photocopier to return to full size.

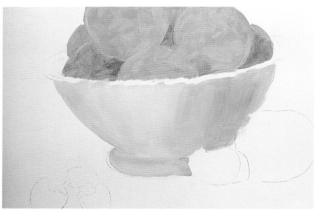

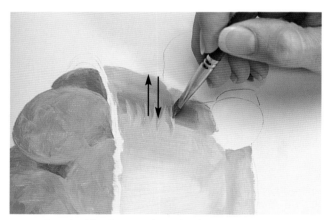

1 Base in the apples with Yellow Ochre plus Cadmium Green Pale. Start to shade the darkest areas of the apple cluster using Cadmium Green Pale plus a little Ivory Black. Block in the colander from dark to light using the color swatches on page 113. Don't try to keep each color within the lines. As I block in the colander, I don't worry if some of my paint gets into the apple area. (I painted the colander before the apples in the front because it is more important to the design than the front apples.)

2 Refine the blending on the colander. An easy way to blend two values that have been laid side by side is to chisel through them, moving the brush back and forth, then dry wipe your brush and soften the transition between the two values. This is just the foundation, so don't try to get a finished look with this one application of paint. Remember, start simple then gradually add more.

Materials List

COLOR MIXES

APPLES

Base	**Shade**	**Second Value Shade**	**Light**	**light**	**Highlight**	**Reflected Light**
Yellow Ochre + Cadmium Green Pale	Cadmium Green Pale + Ivory Black	Shade + Permanent Alizarin Crimson	Cadmium Green Pale	Cadmium Green Pale + Lemon Yellow + Titanium White	Ivory Black + Titanium White	Ivory Black + Titanium White + a touch of greens

COLANDER

Darkest Value	**Second Darkest Value**	**Midvalue**	**Second Lightest Value**	**Lightest Value**	**Resting Shadows**
Burnt Umber + Ivory Black + Prussian Blue	Darkest Value + Titanium White	Second Darkest Value + Yellow Ochre + Titanium White	Midvalue + Titanium White	Second Lightest Value + Titanium White	Permanent Alizarin Crimson + Ivory Black

STRAWBERRIES

Base	**Shade**	**Highlight**
Cadmium Red Light + Permanent Alizarin Crimson	Permanent Alizarin Crimson + Ivory Black	Lemon Yellow + Titanium White

SURFACE

This surface is available from Carolyn's Folk Art Studio, P.O. Box 624, Matthews, NC 38106. Phone (704) 847-0487.

WINSOR & NEWTON ARTISAN WATER MIXABLE OILS

- Lemon Yellow
- Yellow Ochre
- Raw Sienna
- Cadmium Red Light
- Permanent Alizarin Crimson
- Prussian Blue
- Titanium White
- Ivory Black
- Burnt Umber

TRADITIONAL OILS

- Cadmium Green Pale

BRUSHES

- no. 4, no. 6, no. 8 and no. 10 sable chisel blenders
- no. 1 round sable liner

ADDITIONAL SUPPLIES

- Delta Ceramcoat Raw Linen acrylic

- 1-inch (2.5cm) sponge brush
- paper towels
- 220-grit wet/dry sandpaper
- Scotch Brand blue tape
- odorless turpenoid
- plastic wrap
- Krylon Matte Finish spray no. 1311
- Krylon Satin Varnish no. 1701
- oil palette
- dark graphite paper
- tracing paper
- ballpoint pen

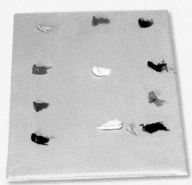

Basecoat the palette board with Raw Linen acrylic.

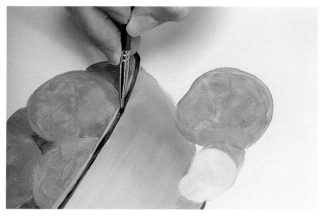

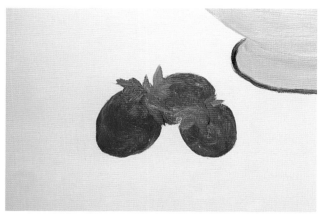

3 Paint the rim of the colander with Ivory Black. Paint the front apples as you did the apples in the colander. Use Cadmium Green Pale plus Titanium White for the apple slice.

4 Base the strawberries with Cadmium Red Light plus Permanent Alizarin Crimson. Base the bracts with the greens from the apples. Once everything is based in, spray dry.

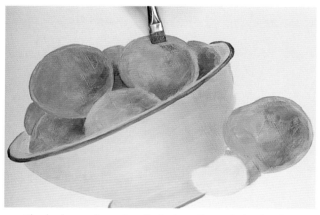

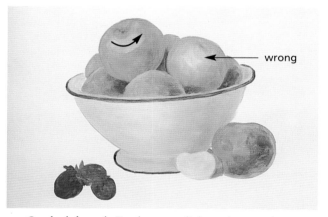

wrong

5 Shade the apples using Cadmium Green Pale plus Ivory Black. Add Permanent Alizarin Crimson and more Ivory Black to this mix for the darkest areas. Keep this color thin and fuzzy.

6 On the left apple I've begun to lighten the area that rounds out. I've reapplied a little base color to help blend and added Cadmium Green Pale plus a little Lemon Yellow. When working on a cool-colored object such as this apple, it's important to have a warmer yellow area in the light area so that the final white highlight will remain clean and pure. The apple on the right had no yellow added to it; the light tone appears milky and hazy.

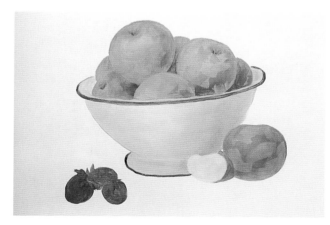

7 Gradually continue to add lighter tones to the apples with more Cadmium Green Pale plus Lemon Yellow plus a little Titanium White. If necessary, pick up some original base color and continue to refine the apples.

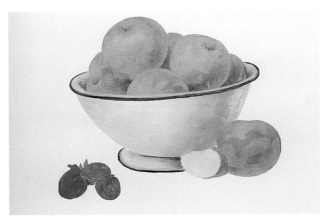

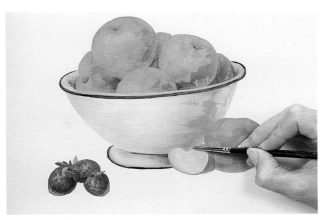

8 Develop the colander further by adding stronger dark areas and lighter light areas. Follow the shape of the colander when applying these mixes. Picking up some of the original base color will help with the blending. After refining the colander, reinforce the black rim area.

9 Detail the strawberries as explained in project seven. Adding some green tints in the strawberries helps them relate to the apples. Add some Raw Sienna to the seed area of the apple slice. Spray dry.

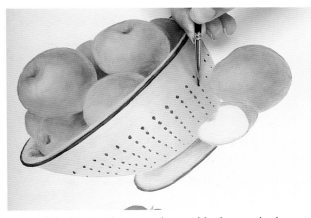

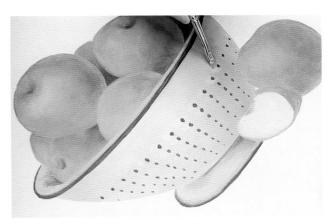

10 After letting the spray thoroughly dry, apply the pattern for the holes by placing the tracing and graphite paper back over the colander. Paint in the holes using a small brush and Ivory Black. As the holes move away from you they become smaller and more oval shaped.

11 Add some light tones around the left side of the holes that are in the front. Keep this soft.

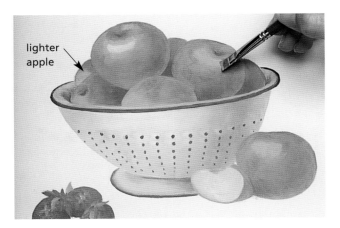

lighter apple

12 Now that I have the colander refined, I can see that I need to further develop the apples. I've added more highlights, concentrating on creating roundness. Notice the apples that are in the very back of the colander—toward the left side they are lighter than the apples in front of them because of the way the light hits the still life.

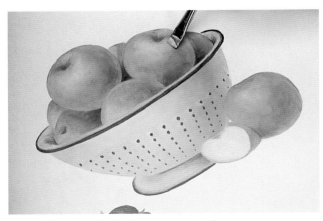

13 Blend the highlight out, creating form.

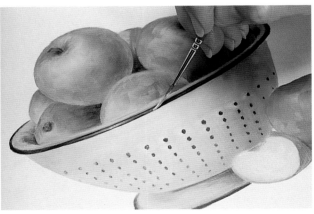

14 Paint the stem in the apple using Raw Sienna plus Ivory Black. Add the shine on the black rim with a liner brush and Titanium White. This shine should gradually diminish as the colander moves away from you.

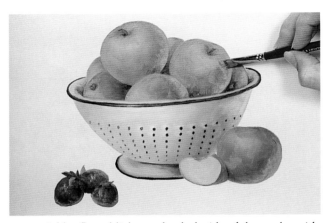

15 Add reflected light on the dark side of the apples with Ivory Black plus Titanium White plus a touch of light green. Keep this thin and splotchy. Spray dry.

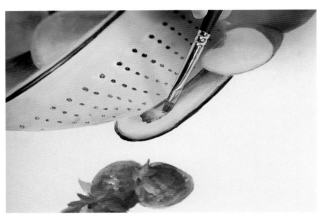

16 Dry brush strawberry color accents on the the left side of the colander and apple colors on the right side. Create a chip and rust stains on the colander by applying Burnt Umber plus a little Raw Sienna.

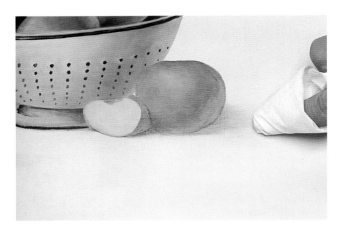

17 Place resting shadows under the strawberries, colander and apples with Permanent Alizarin Crimson plus Ivory Black. With a soft cloth, soften the color so that it gradually diminishes.

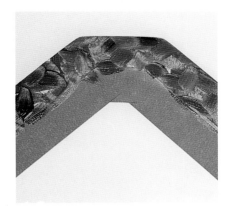

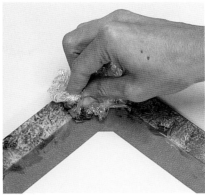

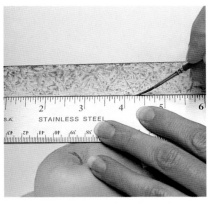

18 To create the border, mark off 1 inch (2.5cm) from all outside edges. Tape this off using blue painter's tape. Using the back of a spoon, press firmly to the edges so that no paint can seep under. Thin down the mixes from your painting with odorless turpenoid: Cadmium Green Pale and Ivory Black; Yellow Ochre and Cadmium Green Pale; Cadmium Green Pale and Permanent Alizarin Crimson. Place these colors on randomly and very splotchy.

19 Next, take a piece of plastic wrap and crinkle it up. Press and twist the plastic wrap into the wet paint.

20 Using a liner brush and a ruler as a guide, paint a small dark green stripe between the border and the background.

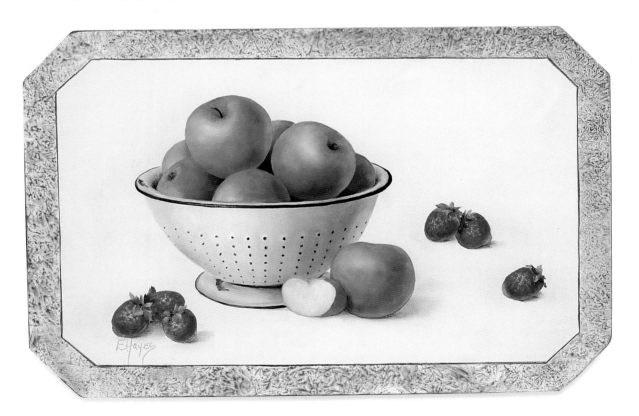

21 Varnish and enjoy.

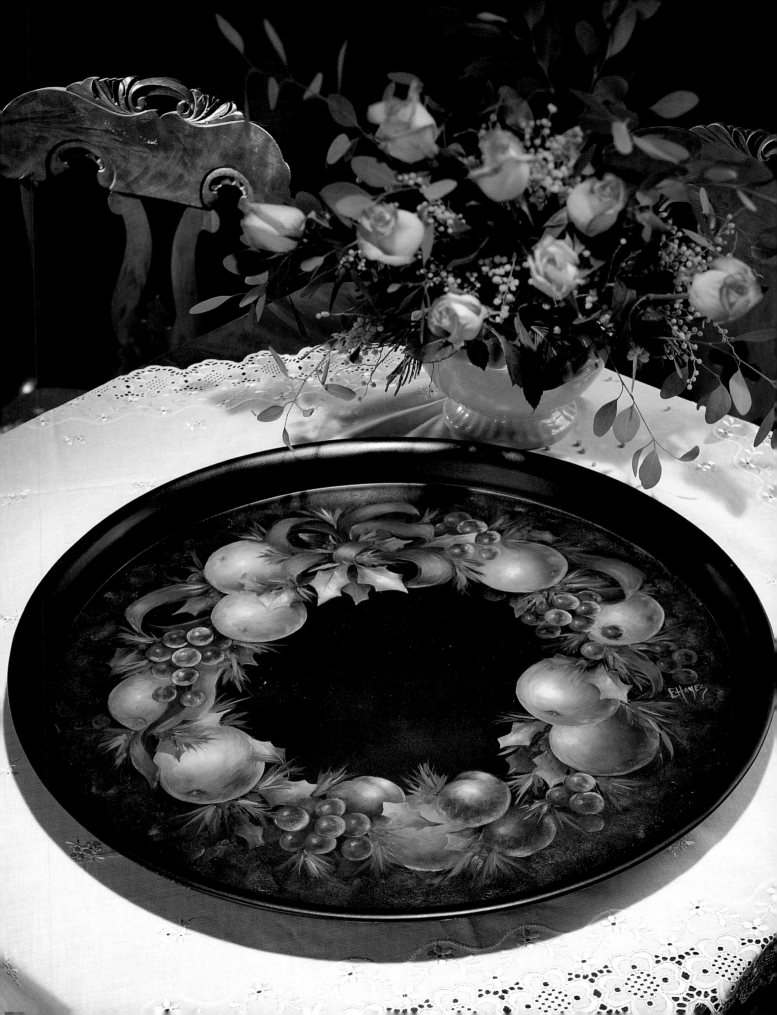

Fruit Wreath

PULLING IT ALL TOGETHER

It's easy to be overwhelmed when you think about all the things that you have to remember when painting. As you continue to paint and your experiences increase, each technique I've talked about will become easier to utilize in your paintings.

As the saying goes, Rome wasn't built in a day and neither is a good painting. Your development and ability to understand and grasp different painting techniques will continue to grow as you strive to do a little better each time.

How Much Detail?

Each element of a design shouldn't receive the same amount of detail. As we focus on an object, that object is in our direct line of vision and is in focus. Objects that appear in our peripheral vision are less focused.

As you paint, concentrate on giving a lot of attention and detail to elements that are the focal point, and as elements move away from the focal point use less detail.

Little filler leaves and elements that are far back in the design should not receive as much detail as focal point elements and leaves.

Don't Be Overwhelmed

When tackling a project that is this involved, don't get so overwhelmed that you find yourself frustrated. Take it step-by-step and day-by-day. This piece is no harder than some of the beginning pieces we did in this book; it just has more elements to it.

When you find yourself getting tired, it's time to stop. Tomorrow is another day and you'll always find time to paint if you really enjoy it.

Stand up, take a break and walk away. Nothing improves your ability to sense what is wrong with a painting better than getting away from it for a while.

Stand Back

As decorative painters we tend to work up close with our paintings and can't see the overall picture. By standing up and moving away from your piece you can judge more accurately what needs more attention. Taking a break will give your eyes and senses a chance to relax. A fresh look will give you a better perspective on what is right and wrong with your painting.

Preparing the Background

Basecoat the tray with Black acrylic following the instructions in chapter two. Transfer the design.

Materials List

SURFACE
This surface is available from Carolyn's Folk Art Studio, P.O. Box 624, Matthews, NC 38106. Phone (704) 847-0487.

WINSOR & NEWTON ARTISAN WATER MIXABLE OILS
- Lemon Yellow
- Yellow Ochre
- Raw Sienna
- Cadmium Red Light
- Permanent Alizarin Crimson
- Cadmium Orange
- Prussian Blue
- Titanium White
- Ivory Black

TRADITIONAL OILS
- Cadmium Green Pale
- Oxide of Chromium

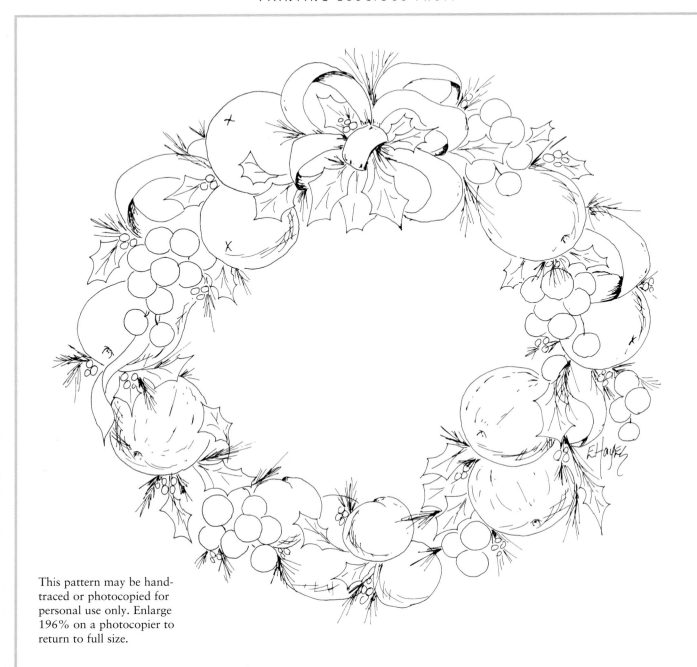

This pattern may be hand-traced or photocopied for personal use only. Enlarge 196% on a photocopier to return to full size.

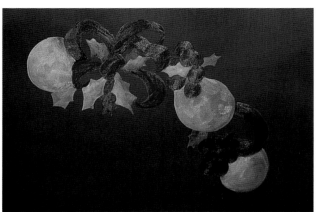

1 Base in the ribbon with Permanent Alizarin Crimson, the leaves with various values and temperatures of Ivory Black plus Oxide of Chromium Green plus a little Lemon Yellow plus Titanium White. Base the oranges with Yellow Ochre plus Cadmium Orange, the grapes with Permanent Alizarin Crimson plus Ivory Black, the pears with Yellow Ochre plus Raw Sienna. Don't add any of the pine needles or little berries at this point. Think about all the skills we have talked about in this book: working in clusters, creating an out-of-focus look, basing elements in various values and temperatures and using values that are in relationship to the background.

Materials List continued

COLOR MIXES

RIBBON

Base	**Shade**	**Light**	**Highlight**
Permanent Alizarin Crimson	Permanent Alizarin Crimson + Ivory Black	Cadmium Red Light + Permanent Alizarin Crimson	Cadmium Red Light + Titanium White

ORANGE

Base	**Shade**	**Light**	**Highlight**
Cadmium Orange + Yellow Ochre	Raw Sienna + Ivory Black + a little Prussian Blue	Cadmium Orange	Light + Lemon Yellow + Titanium White

GRAPES

Base	**Shade**	**Light**	**Highlight**
Permanent Alizarin Crimson + Ivory Black	Base + Ivory Black	Cadmium Red Light + Titanium White	Titanium White

PEARS

Base	**Shade**	**Second Value Shade**	**Light**	**Highlight**
Yellow Ochre + Raw Sienna	Raw Sienna + Ivory Black + a little Permanent Alizarin Crimson	Shade + Permanent Alizarin Crimson	Yellow Ochre	Yellow Ochre + a little Lemon Yellow + Titanium White

PLUMS

PLUMS   ALL

Base	**Shade**	**Light**	**Tints**
Ivory Black + Titanium White + Prussian Blue	Ivory Black + Prussian Blue	Base + Titanium White	Ivory Black + Titanium White + Prussian Blue

LEAVES

Various mixtures of Ivory Black + Prussian Blue, and Oxide of Chromium + Lemon Yellow + Titanium White

BRUSHES

- no. 4, no. 6, no. 8 and no. 10 sable chisel blenders
- no. 1 round sable liner

ADDITIONAL SUPPLIES

- Delta Ceramcoat Black acrylic
- metallic gold oil paint
- 1-inch (2.5cm) sponge brush
- paper towels
- 220-grit wet/dry sandpaper
- odorless turpenoid
- Krylon Matte Finish spray no. 1311
- Krylon Satin Varnish no. 1701
- oil palette
- light graphite paper
- tracing paper
- ballpoint pen

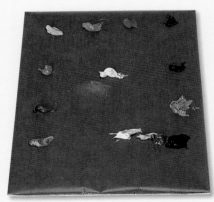

Basecoat the palette board with Black acrylic.

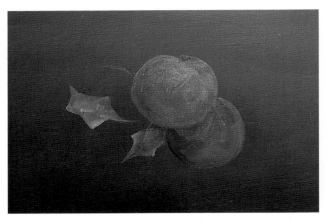

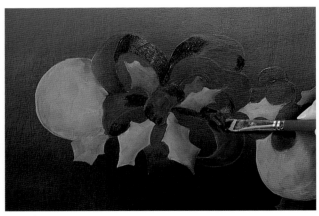

2 Base in the plums with Ivory Black, Prussian Blue plus a little Titanium White. Base in the apples as explained in project five. After everything is based in, spray dry.

3 Shade the ribbon using Permanent Alizarin Crimson plus Ivory Black.

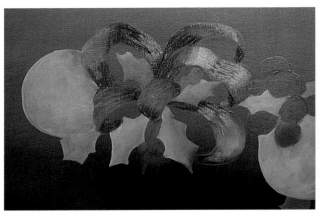

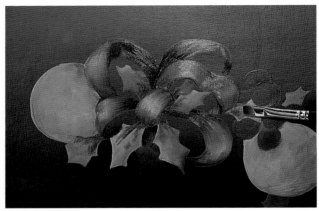

4 Place a lighter value in the ribbon in the most obvious light area with Permanent Alizarin Crimson plus Cadmium Red Light. Using the chisel end of your brush, chisel back and forth between the light area and the dark area. Next, add stronger light areas by using Cadmium Red Light plus Titanium White. Chisel where the two values meet. Soften the chisel marks with a dry wiped brush.

5 Finish refining the ribbon, then add the dark areas to the leaves by using values that are appropriate for each leaf.

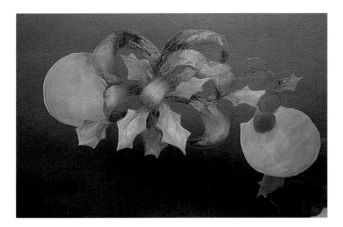

6 Highlight the leaves using different values and temperatures. The leaves in the front are warmer and brighter; the leaves that move further back in the design are darker, cooler and duller.

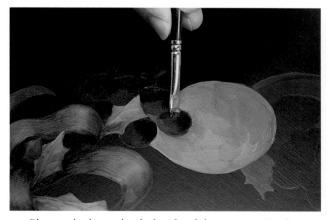

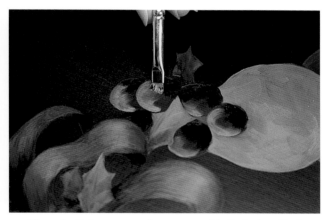

7 Place a shade on the dark side of the grapes using Permanent Alizarin Crimson plus Ivory Black. Fuzz this color out into the middle area. These same colors were used for the base; by adding a touch more Ivory Black you will create the shade mixture.

8 Place the light area on the grapes with Cadmium Red Light plus Titanium White, then start to blend this light tone into the middle area.

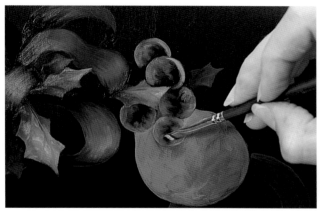

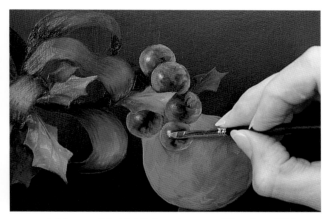

9 Add some reflected light on the dark side of the grapes using Ivory Black, Titanium White and Prussian Blue. Keep this color dry and splotchy.

10 Add a sparkle highlight using pure Titanium White. Don't blend this out too much; just soften the outside edges of the sparkle, keeping the center clean and pure.

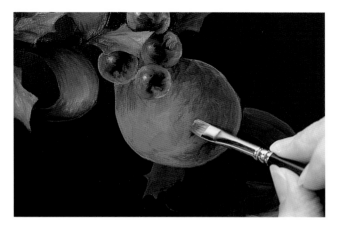

11 Shade the pears using Raw Sienna plus Ivory Black plus a little Permanent Alizarin Crimson. Fuzz this color out into the middle area.

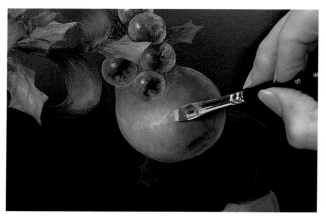

12 Begin highlighting the pear by gradually adding more light tones. Start by applying Yellow Ochre. Blend this tone out. Add a little Lemon Yellow plus Titanium White to the Yellow Ochre for a stronger highlight.

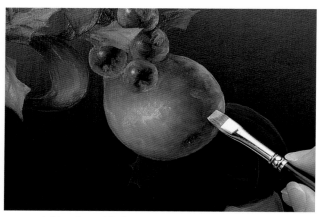

13 Add reflected light using Ivory Black, Titanium White and a touch of Prussian Blue.

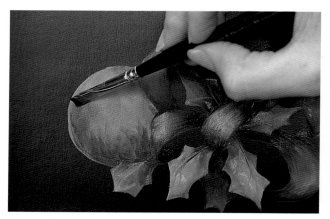

14 Shade the orange using Raw Sienna, Ivory Black and a little Prussian Blue.

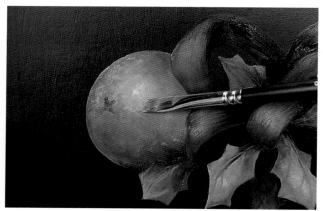

15 Begin to add lighter tones gradually using Cadmium Orange. Then add Lemon Yellow plus Titanium White to the Cadmium Orange. Don't overblend the oranges. To create their texture you need to keep it choppy.

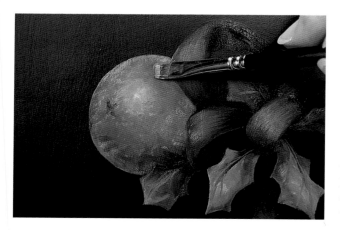

16 Add reflected light using Ivory Black, Titanium White and a touch of Prussian Blue. As you can see, I've worked with the top, main cluster first. Continue around the wreath developing each cluster in this manner.

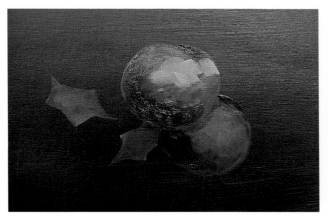

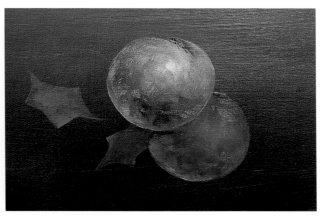

17 Shade the plums using Ivory Black plus Prussian Blue. Add a little more Titanium White to the plum base color and begin to highlight the top plum by placing the color across the fattest part of the plum.

18 Refine the blending and add reflected light to the plums. Notice that the top plum has more contrast than the bottom plum. This helps create depth.

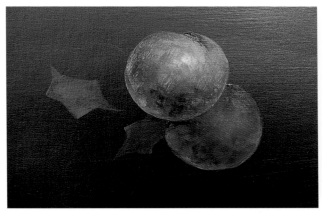

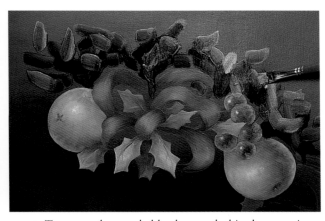

19 Since the plums are blue, which is the coolest color on the color wheel, I've added some warm tints to them with Cadmium Orange plus Yellow Ochre. This helps relate the plums to the warmer elements in the design. Finish developing each cluster in the wreath. Refer to "Apples All Around" for detailed instructions for the apples. Spray dry.

20 To create the mottled background, thin down various dark green mixes from the leaves using odorless turpenoid. Also thin down some metallic gold oil paint with turpenoid. Randomly place these mixes on, keeping them splotchy.

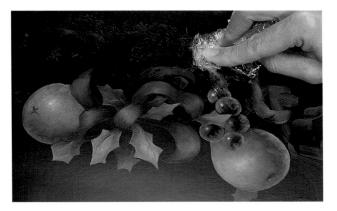

21 Wrinkle up a piece of plastic wrap and press and twist the colors together. If some of the mottling gets into your painting, simply take a kneaded eraser and erase the paint (another advantage to spray drying). I painted this mottled background after I had painted the wreath for two reasons. First, it was an afterthought. Second, by painting it after I had painted the wreath I could easily use colors that were already mixed on my palette, instead of trying to decide what colors I would be using in the wreath.

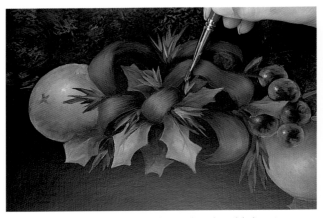

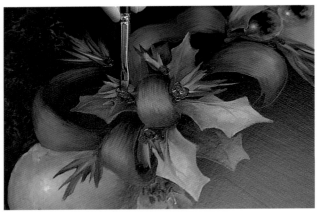

22 Using the chisel edge of your brush, add the pine needles using the thinned down greens that you used in the mottled background. Start off dark and gradually get lighter.

23 Base in the little berries using Alizarin Crimson. No need for a pattern here, just wing it.

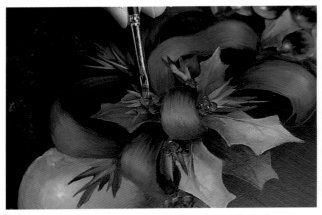

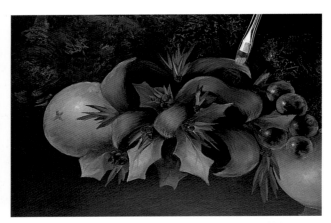

24 Add some light tones to the berries with Cadmium Red Light. Don't get too involved with these berries. They are not the focal point so they don't get much detail.

25 When analyzing, I realized I had added cool blue tints to all the fruit, but the ribbon looked like it was missing something. By adding cool blue tints to the ribbon it helps harmonize everything.

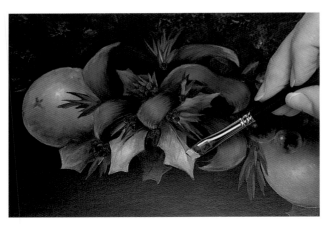

26 Stand back and analyze again. Does anything need lighter lights or darker darks? Here I've strengthened the two front leaves to create more attention to this area.

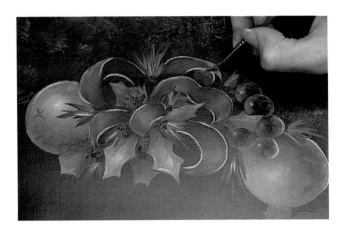

27 I'm always asking myself what else I can do to make my painting sparkle. I decided to add some gold metallic accents by using a liner brush and thinning down the paint with some odorless turpenoid. Don't try to perfectly outline each element. Be free with your hand and let the brush go where it may. Can you see that there are lost and found areas within the gold metallic areas as well? Very important!

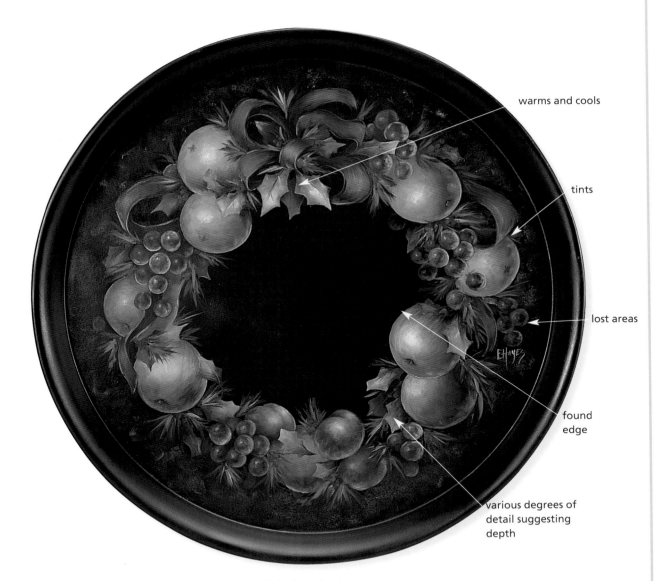

warms and cools

tints

lost areas

found edge

various degrees of detail suggesting depth

28 Wow! This painting makes quite a statement. Sit back and enjoy your accomplishments. All these techniques can be overwhelming at first, but step-by-step, project-by-project, day-by-day you will increase your skills as a decorative artist. You only need to impress yourself. If you are happy with the results then it was a total success. Good luck!

Index